MECHANIC MOTOR VEHICLE FIRST YEAR MCQ

MECHANIC MOTOR VEHICLE FIRST YEAR MCQ

MANOJ DOLE

Made with ♥ on the Notion Press Platform
www.notionpress.com

Digitization is the need of the time. In the future, training in industrial training institutes will need to be conducted using online internet to make training more convenient and easy. E-books containing a set of MCQ questions will be made available to the trainees as they need to be more accustomed to the multiple choice questions MCQ to prepare for the online exams taking place in their industrial training institutes.

With all these factors in mind, Mr. Manoj Madhukar Dole Instructor, Industrial Training Institute, Satara, has written books according to the new annual system and NSQF-5 syllabus. And they've created theoretical mobile apps and blogs to make training easier, and made all these educational materials available for download on the world famous websites Google Play Store, Amazon and Apple Book Store.

The books were published by Hon'ble Joint Director Shri Rajendra Ghume Saheb Regional Office of Vocational Education and Training, Pune on 9/1/2019, at this time Shri Prakash Saigavkar Saheb Principal Government Industrial Training Institute Aundh Pune, Shri Tukaram Misal Saheb Principal Govt. Q. Sanstha Satara, Shri Sachin Dhumal Saheb District Vocational Education and Training Officer Satara, Shri Yatin Pargaonkar Saheb Principal Govt. Q. Sanstha Kolhapur, Shri Vikas Teke Saheb Inspector Vocational Education and Training Regional Office Pune, Palekar Foods Products Pvt. Ltd. Entrepreneurial Chairman of Satara Mr. Nilkanthrao Palekar Saheb, Chairman of Hira Foods Mr. Ibrahim Baba Tamboli Saheb, Mrs. Shalmali Pawar Headmaster Government Technical School Center Satara and other dignitaries were present on the occasion.

Contents

Prologue

Mechanic Motor Vehicle MMV First Year is a simple Book for ITI Engineering Course Mechanic Motor Vehicle (MMV) , First Year, Revised NSQF Syllabus, It contains objective questions with underlined & bold correct answers MCQ covering all topics including all about safety aspect in general and specific to the trade, tools & equipment, raw materials, Measuring & marking by using various Measuring & Marking tools, basic fastening and fitting operations, basics of electricity, electrical parameter, maintenance of batteries, various welding joints by using Arc and gas welding, hydraulics and pneumatics components, Air and Hydraulic Brake system, Diesel Engine of LMV, Cylinder Head , valve train , Piston, connecting rod assembly, crankshaft, flywheel and mounting flanges, spigot and bearings, camshaft, Cooling, lubrication, Intake & Exhaust system of Engine, diesel fuel system, FIP, Governor and monitor emission of vehicle, Starter, alternator and perform Execute troubleshooting in engine of LMV/ HMV and lots more.

We add new question answers with each new version. Please email us in case of any errors/omissions.

Foreword

Vocational education and training is imparted through the Department of Vocational Education and Training through the Department of Business Education and Business Practical to supply multi-skilled artisans in line with the rapidly growing demand in the industrial sector in the 21st century. All the occupations within the institutions are important, as the trainees from these occupations develop multi-skills as per the demands of the industry.

with the noble intention of making available MCQ e-books suitable for all businesses, considering that all the examinations in all thc industries in the industrial sector are conducted online and include MCQ method questions. Mr. Manoj Madhukar Dole has written a very good e-book on MCQ method as per the new annual syllabus. This e-book will definitely be a guide for all the trainees, trainee candidates, training instructors and others concerned.

The author of the book is Mr. Manoj Madhukar Dole, Instructor Gov. ITI Satara has 17 years of training experience. Written as a new annual pattern, this e-book incorporates modern digital QR Code technology to understand the layout, simple language, and simple syntax, diagrams and videos for each subject. So I am sure that this e-book will definitely be useful for in-depth study and exam practice. The work they have done is certainly commendable.

Mr. Tukaram Misal
Principal Government Industrial Training Institute Satara.

Preface

DGET New Delhi and CSTARI Kolkata have been implementing an annual pattern for all businesses in ITI since the August 2018 session. The examination system will also be changed and it will be online from this year and since all the questions are of Objective Type (MCQ), the trainees are in dire need of in-depth study. It is with this in mind that we are delighted to present the books based on the old NIMI pattern and a complete overview of the new annual pattern, and we hope that these books will be a guide for all business directors and trainees. Is.

For writing these books, Johar Awate Saheb, Principal of ITI Akluj. Former Principal of ITI Satara Saigavkar Saheb, Assistant Director Shri Chandrakant Dhekne Saheb Regional Office of Vocational Education and Training, Pune, District Vocational Education and Training Officer Sachin Dhumal Saheb and Headmaster Government Technical School Kendra Shalmali Pawar Madam and son Adhiraj Dole, mother Kusum Dole, I am very grateful to my father Madhukar Dole and wife Ashwini Dole for their special guidance and cooperation from time to time.

Also, in a very short period of time, the book was reviewed by Shri Rajendra Ghume Saheb, Joint Director, Vocational Education and Training Regional Office, Pune, for his invaluable time in publishing the book. I am sincerely grateful for their feedback.

I am grateful to the Instructor of ITI Satara for there continuous support from the very beginning of writing the book.

From this book, I consider myself blessed to have shared my thoughts on e-learning with you. I will not claim that this book is perfect, because considering the perfection, this book is an attempt and is in its infancy. They will be valuable for improvement if they are tested and suggested.

Manoj Dole
Dated 9/1/2019

Acknowledgements

The industrial training and theoretical examination system of our industrial training institutes and these changes have been accepted by the craft instructors and the trainees. Theoretical examinations conducted in your industrial training institutes are also conducted online. Since these examinations are of multiple choice MCQ method, the trainees will need to get more practice of such questions.

With all these considerations in mind, Mr. Manoj Madhukar, Director, Dole Crafts, Katari Industrial Training Institute, Satara, has done a thorough study and with his diligent work and added his keen intellect, according to the new annual system and NSQF-5 syllabus, e-book of Katari and other machine trades. -Book) and they have created mobile apps and blogs on theoretical topics to make training easier and have made all these educational materials available for download on the world famous websites Google Play Store, Amazon and Apple Book Store. Training has been made easier by creating a print version and using advanced techniques like QR Code.

All these educational materials will definitely be a guide for all the trainees for in-depth study and for the craft instructors and other concerned who are imparting vocational training.

CHAPTER ONE

Mechanic Motor Vehicle First Year MCQ Drawings

Online Test Exam
ITI Books
CNC Course
AutoCAD CAM
JOB & Apprentice
Online Theory
Computer Course
Trading Course
Web Designing
MSCIT Course
Shopping Business
Internet Business
Remotasks Course
Online Services
Top Sportsmans
Indian Army
Freedom Fighters
Top Scientists
Social Reformers
Motivational Speaker
Top Richest People
Join WhatsApp Group
Join Facebook Group
Like Facebook Page
PAN / Adhar / Licence Passport

Fire extinguisher

Calliper

Hacksaw frame

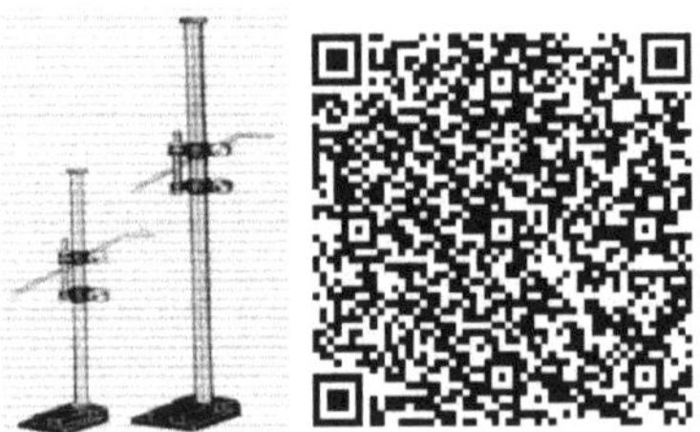

Universal surface guage

Hammer

Centre punch

Bench vice

Files

Scraper

Surface Plate

Outside Micrometer

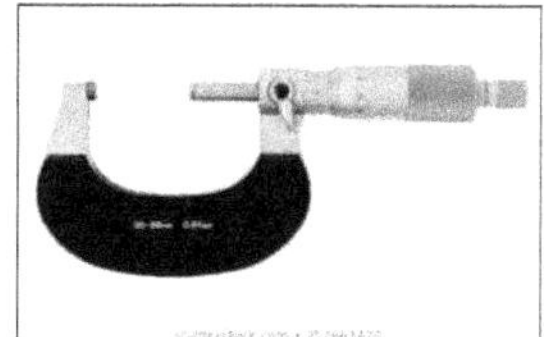

Micrometer

Depth micrometer

Vernier Calliper

Vernier bevel protractor

Drilling

Reamer

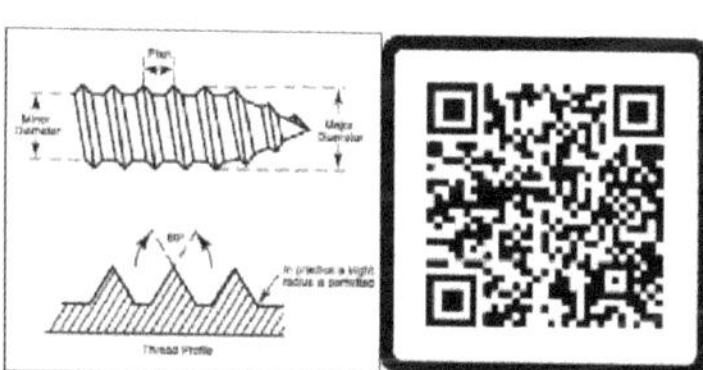

Thread

Tap Die

Grinding Wheel

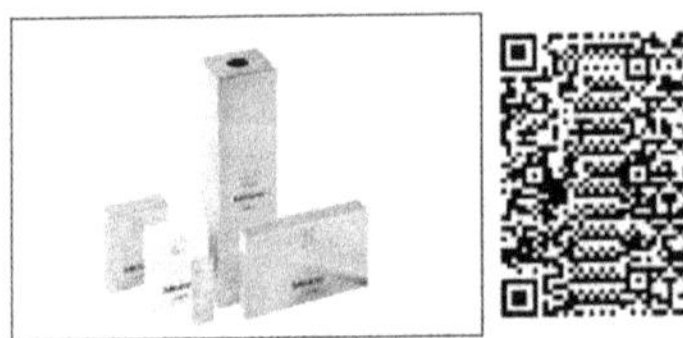

Slip gauge

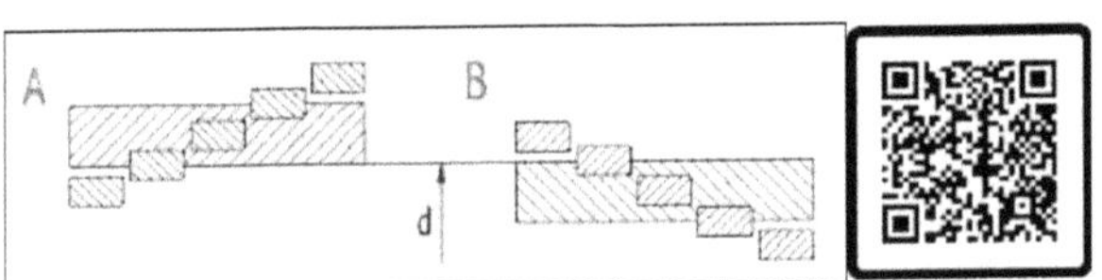

Limit fit tolerance

taper ring gauge

screw pitch gauge

Gear

screw pitch gauge

Tap Die

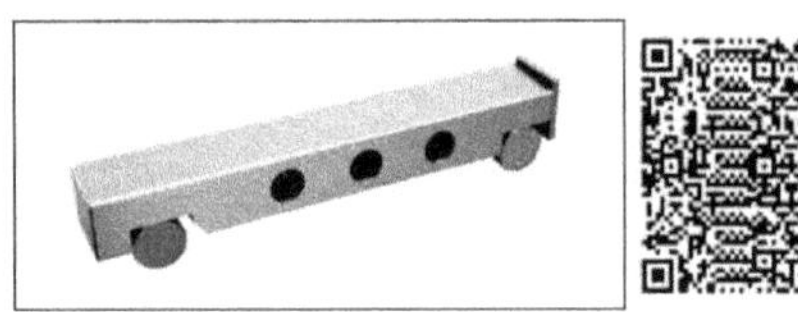

Sine bar

Slip gauge

Dial test indicator

Telescopic gauge

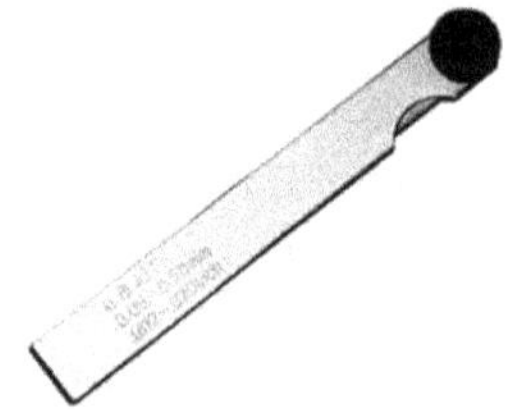

Feeler gauge

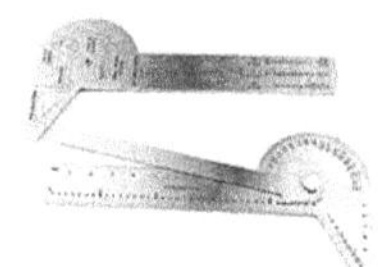

Centre gauge

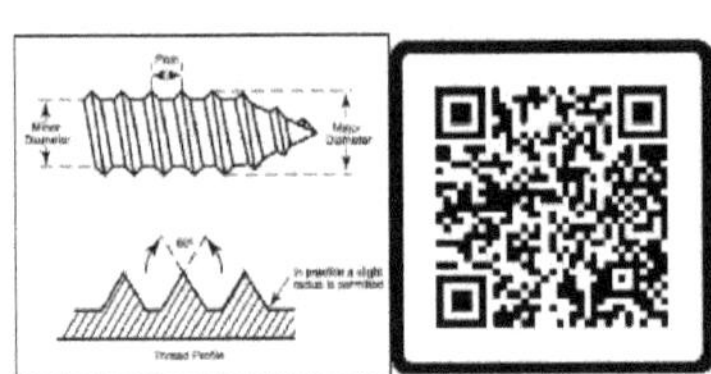

Thread

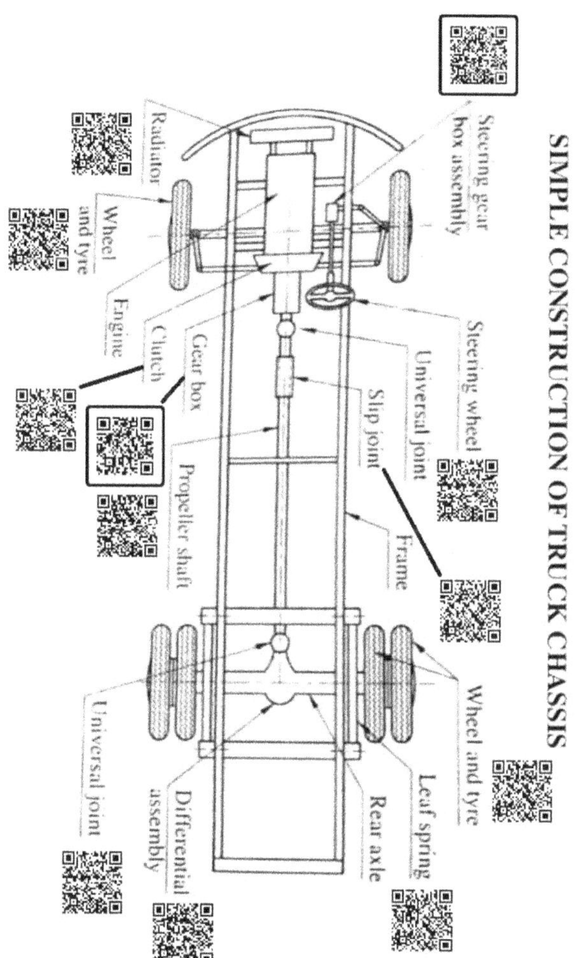
SIMPLE CONSTRUCTION OF TRUCK CHASSIS
Steering gear box assembly
Radiator
Wheel and tyre
Engine
Clutch
Gear box
Steering wheel
Universal joint
Slip joint
Propeller shaft
Frame
Wheel and tyre
Leaf spring
Rear axle
Differential assembly
Universal joint

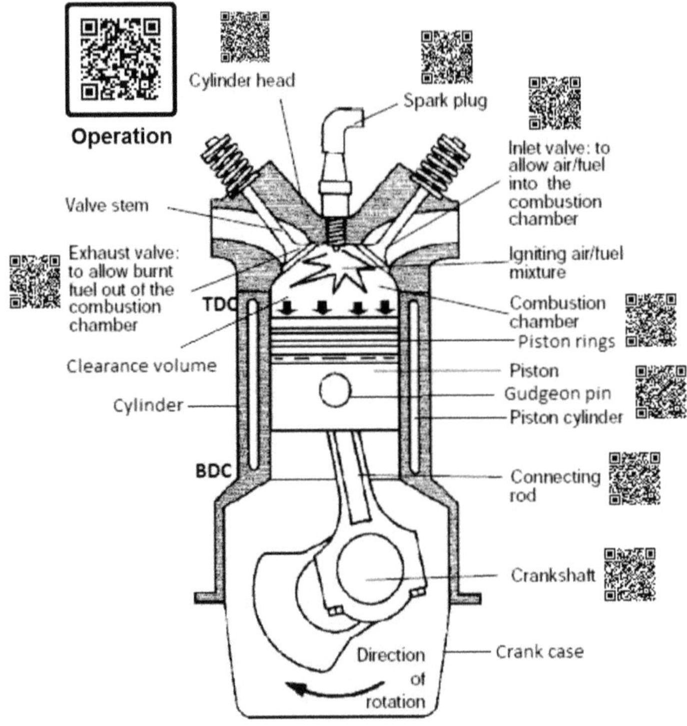

Petrol Engine Details

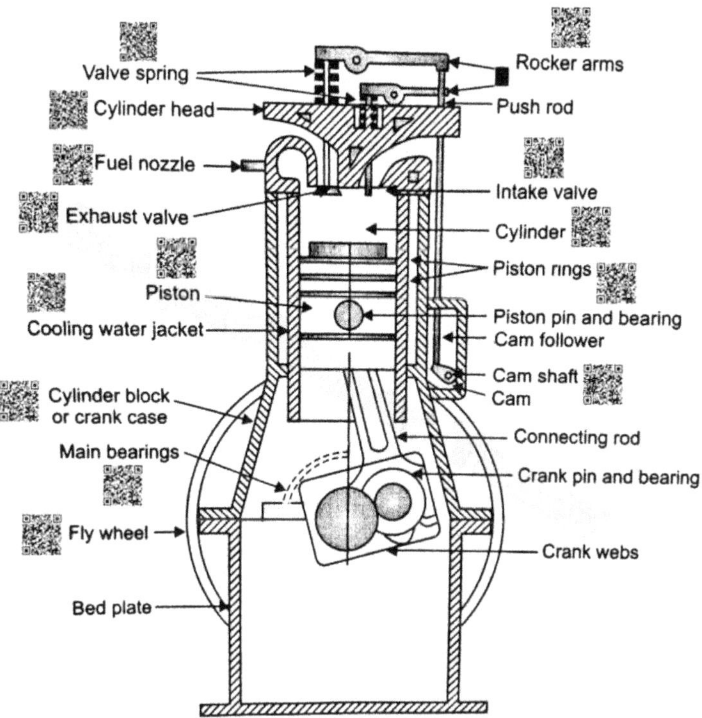

Components of Diesel Engine

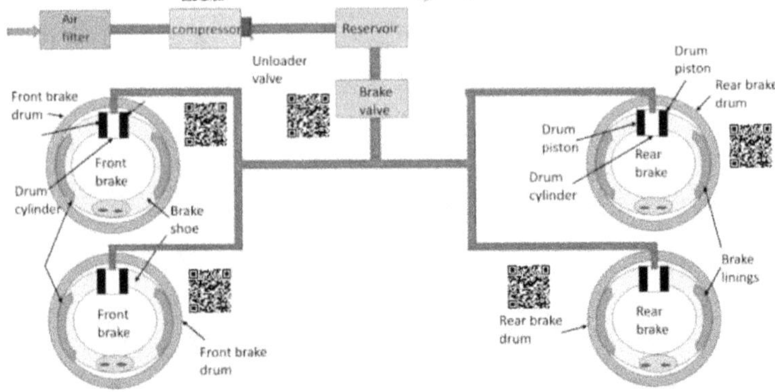
Air Braking system
Air filter
compressor
Reservoir
Unloader valve
Brake valve
Front brake drum
Front brake
Drum cylinder
Brake shoe
Front brake
Front brake drum
Drum piston
Rear brake drum
Drum piston
Drum cylinder
Rear brake
Brake linings
Rear brake drum
Rear brake

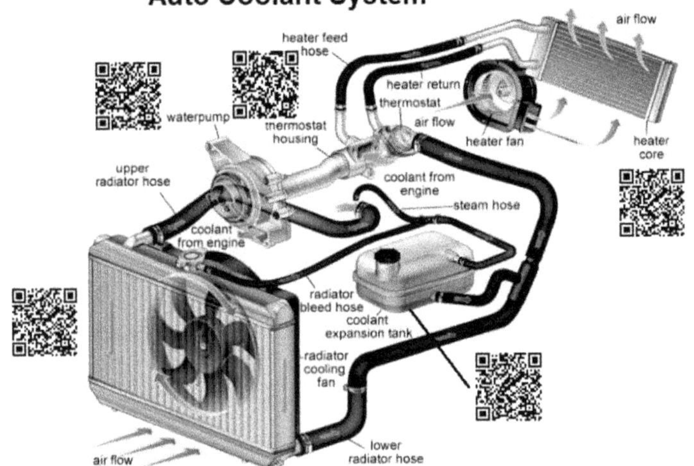
Auto Coolant System
heater feed hose
air flow
heater return
thermostat
air flow
heater fan
heater core
waterpump
thermostat housing
upper radiator hose
coolant from engine
steam hose
coolant from engine
radiator bleed hose
coolant expansion tank
radiator cooling fan
air flow
lower radiator hose

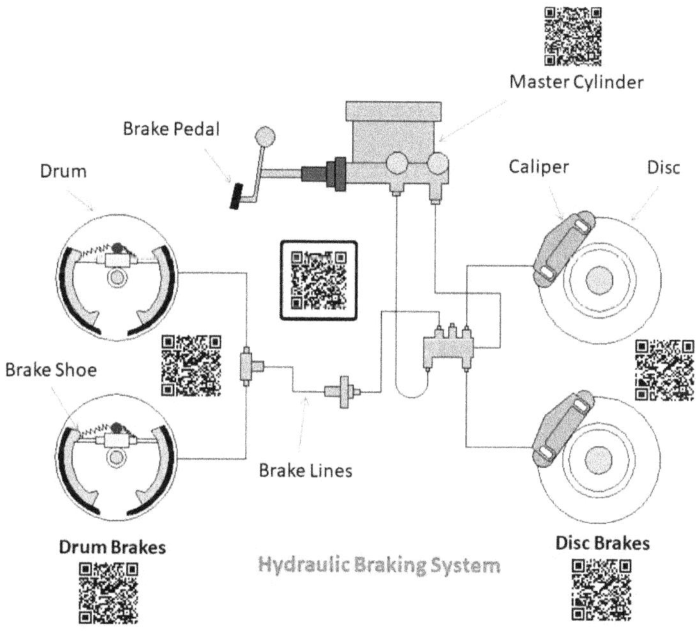
Master Cylinder
Brake Pedal
Drum
Caliper
Disc
Brake Shoe
Brake Lines
Drum Brakes
Hydraulic Braking System
Disc Brakes

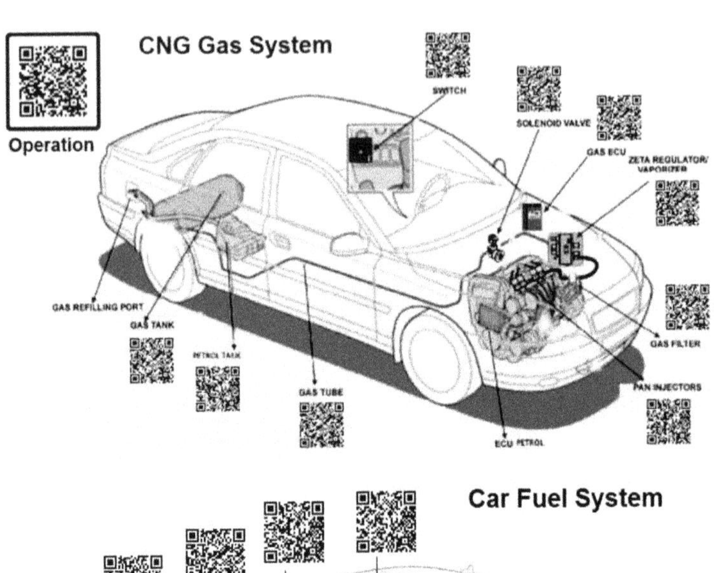
CNG Gas System
Operation
SWITCH
SOLENOID VALVE
GAS ECU
ZETA REGULATOR/
VAPORIZER
GAS REFILLING PORT
GAS TANK
GAS TUBE
GAS FILTER
PAN INJECTORS
ECU PETROL

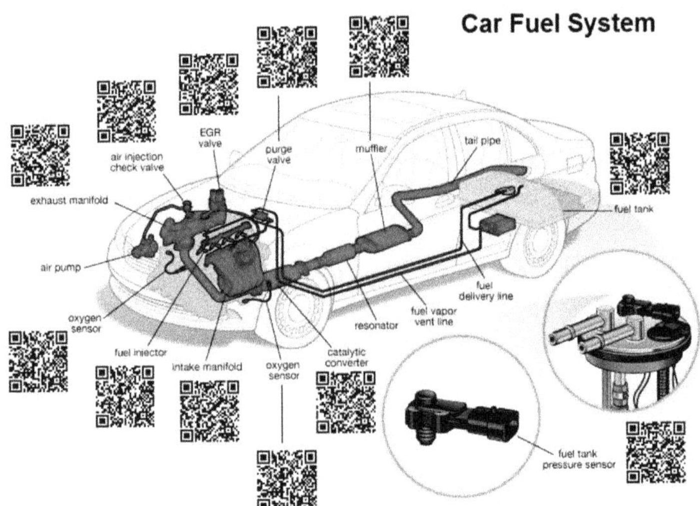
Car Fuel System
EGR valve
air injection check valve
purge valve
muffler
tail pipe
fuel tank
exhaust manifold
air pump
oxygen sensor
fuel injector
intake manifold
oxygen sensor
catalytic converter
resonator
fuel vapor vent line
fuel delivery line
fuel tank pressure sensor

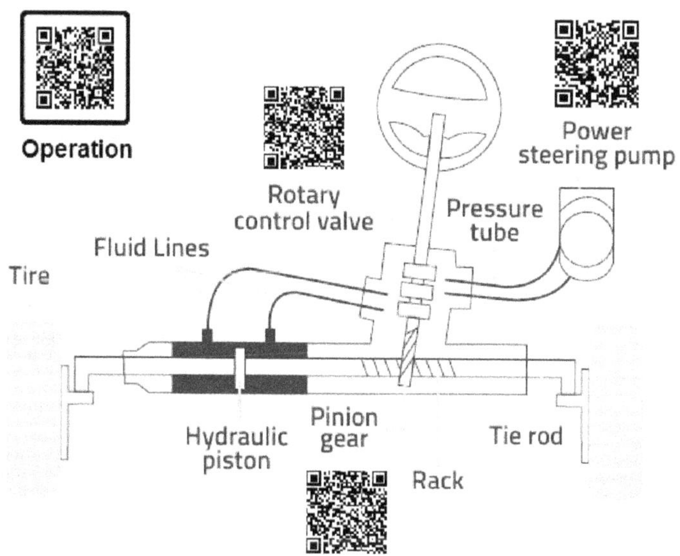

Power Steering System

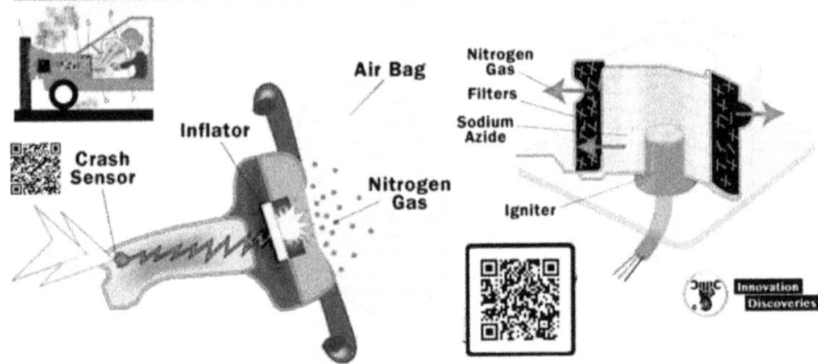
WHAT IS AIRBAG?
HOW IT WORKS DURING AN ACCIDENT?
Air Bag
Inflator
Crash Sensor
Nitrogen Gas
Nitrogen Gas
Filters
Sodium Azide
Igniter
Innovation
Discoveries

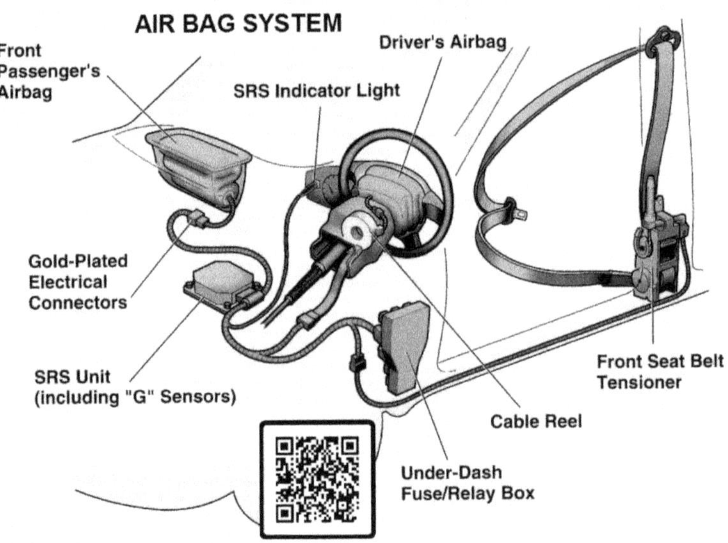
AIR BAG SYSTEM
Front Passenger's Airbag
Driver's Airbag
SRS Indicator Light
Gold-Plated Electrical Connectors
SRS Unit (including "G" Sensors)
Front Seat Belt Tensioner
Cable Reel
Under-Dash Fuse/Relay Box

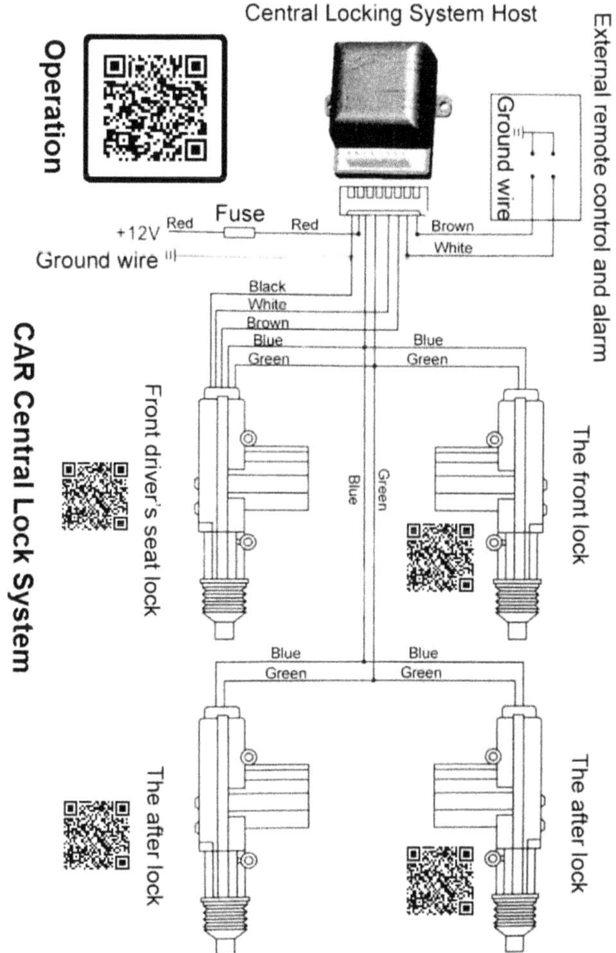
Central Locking System Host
External remote control and alarm
Ground wire
Operation
Fuse
+12V
Red
Red
Brown
White
Ground wire
Black
White
Brown
Blue
Green
Blue
Green
CAR Central Lock System
Front driver's seat lock
The front lock
Blue
Green
Blue
Green
Blue
Green
The after lock
The after lock

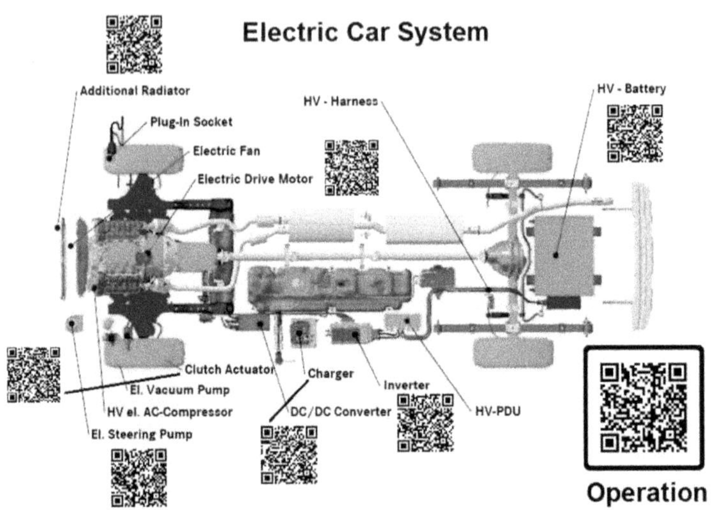

Multi Point Fuel Injection Syastem

D- MPFI & L- MPFI

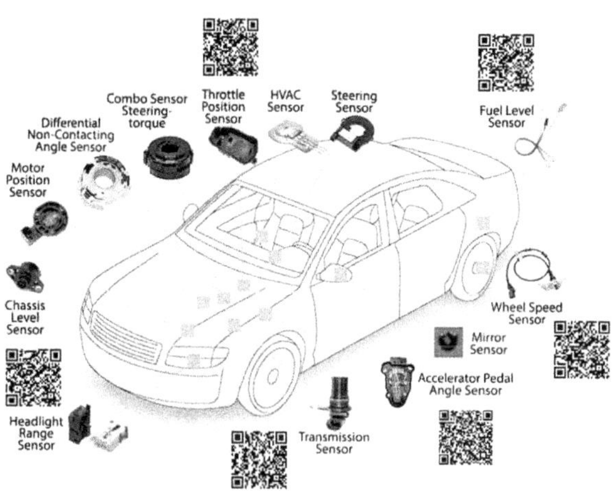

Car Sensor System

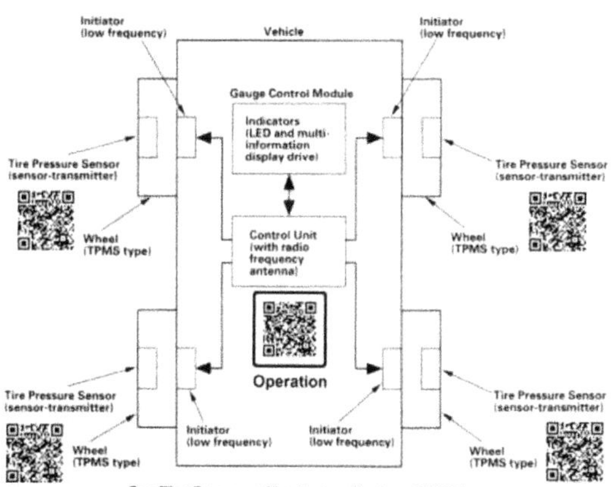

Car Tire Pressure Monitoring System (TPMS)

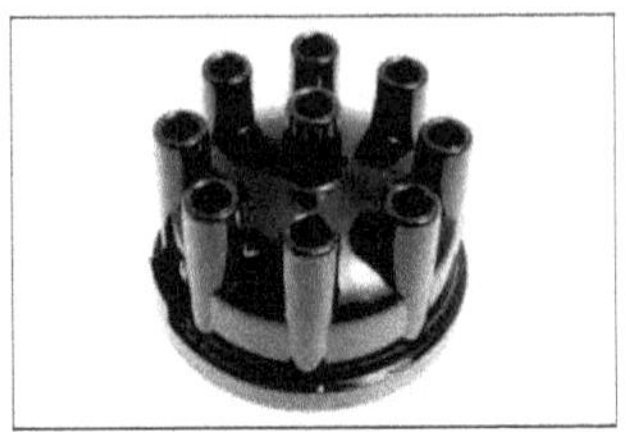

Dynamo (Alternator) distributor cap in car

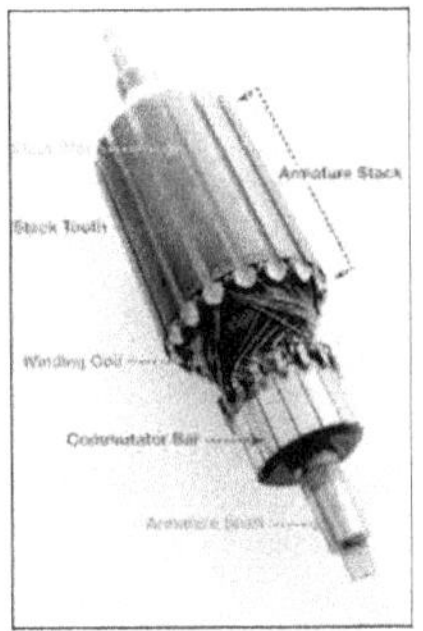

Starter winding armature in vehicle

Air tank safety valve

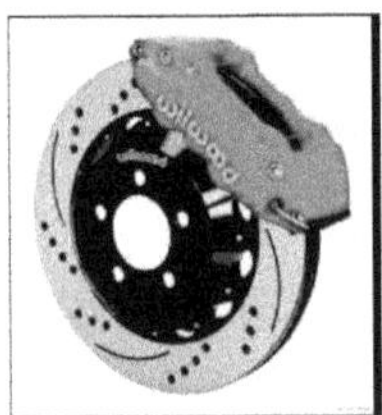

Brakes in car

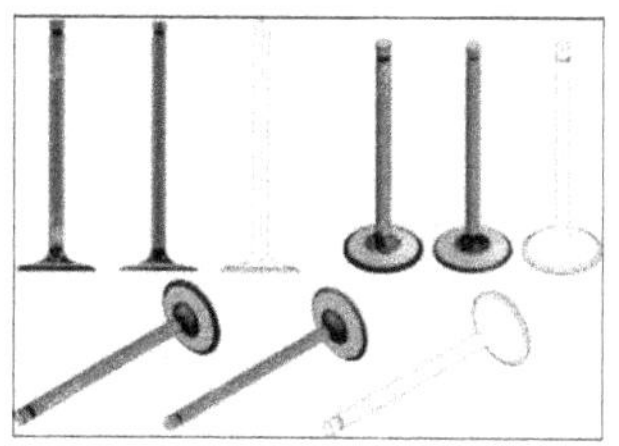

Engine valves

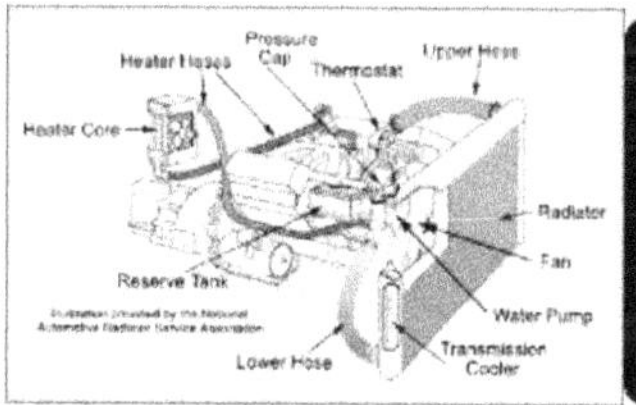

Cooling system in car

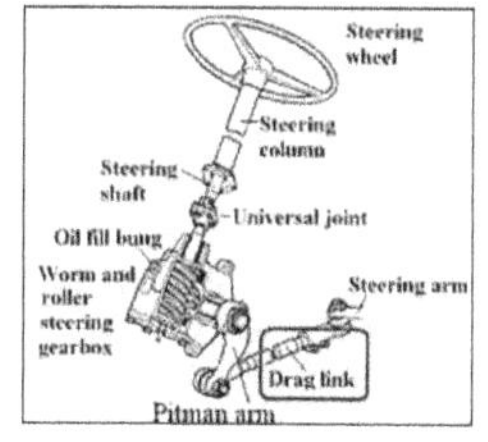

Steering gearbox in vehicle

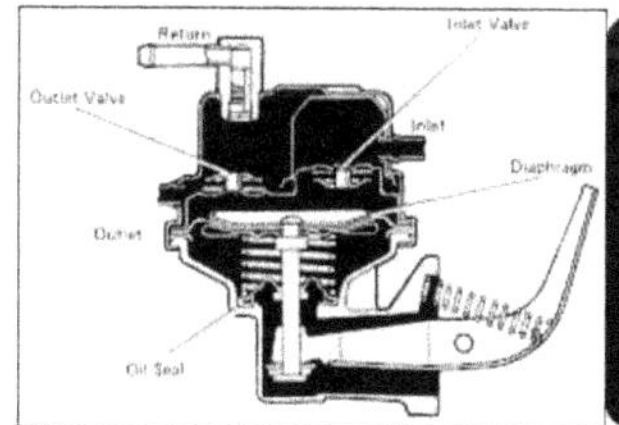

Fuel pump in Vehicle

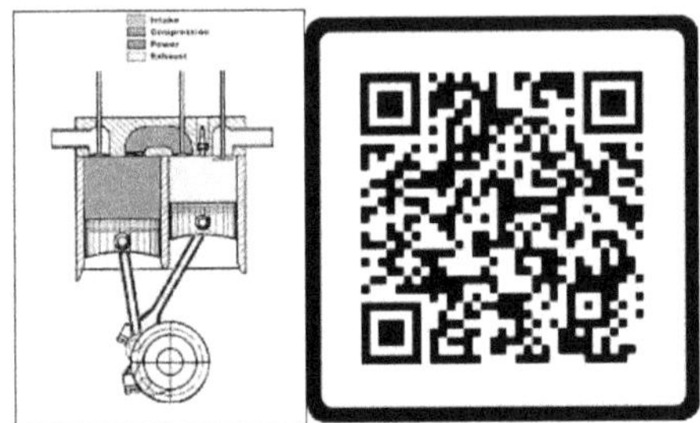

Engine in vehicle

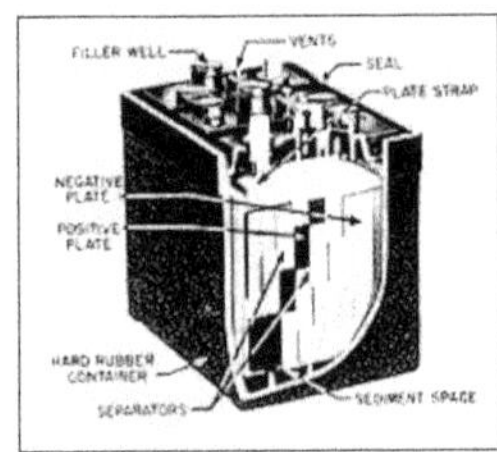

Lead acid battery in vehicle

Piston & rings in Engine

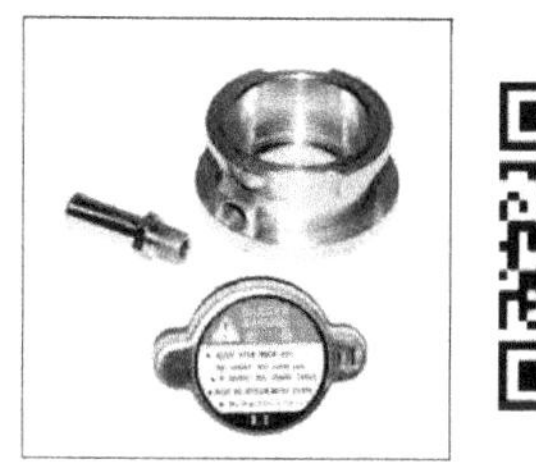

Radiator cap in vehicle

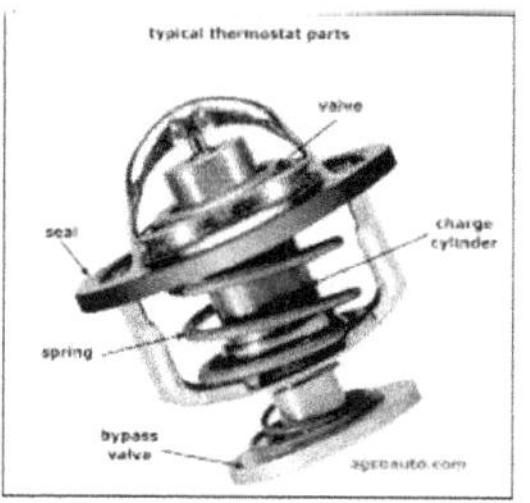

Thermostat valve in vehicle

CHAPTER TWO

Mechanic Motor Vehicle First Year MCQ

01] In case of bleeding, take treatment Of

D] cold 3" and rest

A] spray cold water

B] Bandage immediately -----.

B] Enquire about the accident thought treatment

02] in case of an accident, the victim should im

A] Asked to take rest

C] Attended immediately

D] leave him

03] First aid is given to an injured or ill person primarily....

A] Save life

B] Prevent further deterioration of the muff's

C] Give best possible comfort

D] All of these

04] Colour code for Bins for waste paper segregation is -----

A] Blue Colour

B] Yellow Colour

C] Red Colour

D] Green Colour

05] In Japanese Seiko stands for -------------

A] Shine

B] Sort

C] Standardize

D] Sustain

06] Benefit of SS system is ------

A] Increase in productivity

B] Increase in quality

C] Reduction in wastage of time

D] All of these

07] Safety is -----------

A] Nobody's business

B] Every bodies business

C] Some bodies business

D] The organization business

08] For basic categories of safety signs are available The meaning of "prohibition" sign ----

A] Shows it must not be done

B] Shows what must be done

C] Warns the hazard or danger

D] Gives information of safety provision

09] Which one is a workshop safety?

A] Keep shop floor clean and free from grease, oil or other slippery materials

B] Stop the machine before changing the speed

C] Don't use cracked or chipped tools

D] Don't try to stop a running machine with hand

10] In Personal Protect Equipment (PPE] HELMET is used to

A] Protect head

B] Protect eyes

C] Protect hands

D] Protect ears

11] Which of the following belongs to general safety?

A Have a worker in good attitude

B] The work clean and clear

C] Concentrate on your work

D] Keep the floor and gangways clean and clear

12] While grinding, which is used to protect the eyes?

A] Dark green glass

B] Mask

C] Sun glasses

D] Safety goggles

Grinding

13] Which of the following is done for machine safety?

A] Check the oil level before starting the machine

B] Do things in a methodical way

C] Keep the floor and gangways clean and clear

D] Don't use dies and scarves

14] In Personal Protect Equipment (PPE], 'sleeves' is used to protect ----------

A] Face

B] Eyes

C] Ears

D] Hands

15] ABC stands for --------------

A] Automatic Breathing Control

B] Automatic Blood Control

C] Airway Breathing Circulation

D] Automatic Blood Circulation

16] To put off "Class B" fire, the types of fire extinguisher used is............

A] Dry power

B] Carbon dioxide

C] Jet of water

D] Foam type

17] Which type of fire extinguisher is used to put off general fire?

A] Water type Extinguisher

B] Foam type Extinguisher

C] Dry chemical powder Extinguisher

D] Carbon dioxide (C02] Extinguisher

fire extinguisher

18] One micrometer (U] is equal to...

A] 0.1mm

B] 0.01mm

C] 0.001mm

D] 0.0001mm

19] The calliper meant for measuring the width of a slot is...

A] Odd leg calliper

B] Outside calliper

C] Jenny calliper

D] Inside calliper

20] The size of the dividers are specified by the -----------

A] Total length of legs

B] Distance between the points when fully opened

C] Length of legs without points

D] Distance between the pivot and the point

21] The instrument used to mark parallel lines, parallel to the datum edge is -

A] Jenny caliper

B] Divider

C] Outside calliper

D] Inside calliper

Callipers

22] Which one of the following is an indirect measuring tool?

A] Outside caliper

B] Vernier calliper

C] Steel rule

D] Outside micrometer

23] For cutting thin tubing, the most suitable pitch of the hacksaw blade is...

A] 1.8mm

B] 1.4mm

C] 1mm

D] 0.8mm

24] For cutting solid brass, the most suitable pitch of the hacksaw blade is...

A] 1.8mm

B] 1.4mm

C] 1mm

D] 0.8mm

Hacksaw frame

25] A new hacksaw blade after a few strokes becomes loose because of the...

A] Stretching of the blade

B] Wing-nut threads being worn out

C] Wrong pitch of the blade

D] Improper selection of the set of saws.

26] While cutting small diameter pipes, it is advisable to watch regularly and ensure that...

A] The cut is along the curved line

B] More saw teeth are in contract

C] The work is not overheated

D] Proper balancing of hacksaw is maintained

27] The vice clamps are used to...

A] Protect hard jaws

B] Clamp the work pieces rigidly

C] Protect the finished surfaces

D] Prevent the movable jaw being filed

28] The reference surface during marking is provided by the...

A] Surface gauge

B] Work piece

C] Drawing of the work

D] Marking table surface

29] The size of an engineer's vice is specified by the...

A] Length of the movable jaw

B] Width of the jaws

C] Height of the vice

D] Maximum opening of the jaws

30] Portion of the hammer used for fixing the handle is...

A] Face

B] Peen

C] Cheek

D] Eye hole

31] Weight of the hammer for the marking purpose is...

A] 250g

B] 500g

C] 1 kg

D] 2 kgs

Hammer

32] The size of the dividers are specified by the...

A] Total length of the legs

B] Distance between the points when fully opened

C] Length of legs without the points

D] Distance between the pivot and the point

33] The included angle of the groove of 'V' block is always....

A] 45°

B] 60°

C] 90°

D] 120°

34] 'V' blocks are available in grades of...

A] A & B

B] A,B & C

C] 1,2 & 3

D] 1 & 2

35] 'V' blocks of grade 'B' are made of

A] Cast iron

B] Mild steel

C] Steel

D] Cast steel

36] Name the punch used to locate the centre.

A] Prick punch 30°

B] Prick punch 60°

C] Centre punch

D] Dot punch

centre punch

37] The point angle of centre punch is --------

A] 30°

B] 50°

c] 900

D] 1200

38] Punches are used for forming ---------of any shape

A] Holes

B] Mining

C] Knurling

D] Reaming

39] Generally the length of the handle of the vice is ----------

A] 1.5 times the normal size of the vice

B] 2.5 times the normal size of the vice

C] 3.5 times the normal size of the vice

D] 4.5 times the normal size of the vice

Bench vice

40] Bench vice spindle is made of ....

A] Mild steel
B] Cast iron
C] Tool steel
D] Bronze

41] The part of the universal surface gauge which helps to draw a parallel line along a datum edge is the..
A] Rocker arm
B] Snug
C] Fine adjustment screw
D] Guide pins

42] Scribers are made of...
A] Mild steel
B] High carbon steel
C] Brass
D. Cast iron

43] The point angle of scriber is ----------
A] 30°
B] 60°
C] 5° to 10°
D] 12° to 15°

44] The cutting angle for chipping cast iron is...
A] 37.5°
B] 55°
C] 60°
D] 90°

45] The chisel will dig into the material when...
A] The rake angle is more
B] The clearance angle is too low
C] The angle of inclination is more
D] The angle of inclination is too low

46] A slight convexity is given to the cutting edge to...
A] Cut curved surfaces
B] Cut sharp corners
C] Prevent digging of the ends
D] Allow the lubricant to enter

47] Used on finished tubular wrench surfaces to avoid marking.
A] Stillson pipe
B] Chain wrench

C] Strap wrench

D] Footprint wrench

48] Used for gripping and turning pipes and round stocks in confined places.

A] Stillson pipe

B] Chain wrench

C] Strap wrench

D] Footprint wrench

49] Used for holding iarge diameter pipes.

A] Stillson pipe

B] Chain wrench

C] Strap wrench

D] Footprint wrench

50] Used for gripping and turning pipes,tubes and cylindricai rods.

A] Stillson pipe

B] Chain wrench

C] Strap wrench

D] Footprint wrench

51] in a metric micrometer, a complete revolution of thimble advances -----------

A] 0.01 mm

B] 0.25 mm

C] 0.50 mm

D] 1.00mm

52] Ratchet Stop in the micrometer helps to ------------

A] Control the pressure

B] Lock the spindle

C] Adjust the zero error

D] Hold the work piece

53] 1000 micron means ------------

A] 1 mm

B] 1 m

C] 1000 mm

D] 10 cm

54] What is the zero reading of a 50-75 mm outside micrometer?

A] 0.000 mm

B] 0.01 mm

C] 25.00 mm

D] 50.00 mm

55] The value of the smallest division on sleeve of a metric outside micrometer is -----

A] 0.50 mm

B] 1.00 mm

C] 1.50 mm

D] 2.00 mm

Micrometer

56] Ratchet stop in the micrometer helps to ---------

A] Control the pressure

B] Lock the spindle

C] Adjust the zero error

D] Hold the work piece

Depth micrometer

57] Least count of depth micrometer is

A] 0.5 mm

B] 0.2 mm

C] 0.001 mm

D] 0.01 mm

58] The least count of vernier calliper is (main scale = 49 division, vernier scale = 50 division]

A] 0.1 mm

B] 0.01 mm

C] 0.001 mm

D] 0.02 mm

59] The type of measurement made by using a Vernier Calliper is -------

A] Direct measurement

B] Indirect measurement

C] 90“] (a] 81 (b]

D] None of these

60] Telescopic gauges are used to measure holes and slots.

A] from 10 mm to 100 mm

B] from 12 mm to 152 mm

C] from 12.7 mm to 152.4 mm

D] none of the above.

Telescopic gauge

61] Small hole gauges are used to measure holes and slots.

A] below 10 mm

B] below 12.7 mm

C] below 20 mm

D] below 20.7 mm.

Dial test indicator

62] The dial test indicator shows the measurement as...

A.] The actual size of the component

B.] The difference between the two steps of 5 mm

C.] The magnified small variations in sizes through a pointer

D.] The direct reading of the dimension

63] V -block and dial indicator method is used to measure the

A] Length of the work piece ground

B] Circularity of the surface of the work piece

C] Flatness of the surface

D] Pitch of the thread

64] Which one of the following is not correct about dial test indicator?

A] It has 100 divisions on its dial

B] Motion of the stem is transferred to the dial through Gear train.

C] Its accuracy is 0.1 mm

65] the feeler gauge is used for...

A] Checking surface roughness

B] Checking the radius of work pieces

C] Checking the gap between mating parts

D] Checking the accuracy of the hole locators

Feeler gauge

66] Threading tools are checked for accuracy for the 60◦ angle by using a

A] Thread plug gauge

B] centre gauge

C] screw pitch gauge

D] tool angle gauge

Centre gauge

67] The number of threads per inch can be checked with a

A] tool gauge

B] metric rule by counting

C] ring gauge
D] screw pitch gauge

screw pitch gauge

68] Used where bolt and threads are to be protected from damage.
A] Donald cap nut
B] Thumb nut
C] Hexagonal nut
D] Wing-nut

Thread

69] Used where frequent removal and fixing is required.
A] Donald cap nut
B] Thumb nut
C] Hexagonal nut
D] Wing-nut
70] Used in machine building and structure work.
A] Donald cap nut
B] Thumb nut
C] Hexagonal nut
D] Wing-nut
71] Used where frequent adjustments are to be made.
A] Donald cap nut

B] Thumb nut

C] Hexagonal nut

D] Wing-nut

72] Nylon inserts in the nut prevent loosening.

A] Locking plate

B] Wire lock

C] Self-locking nut

D] Sawn nut

73] A slot is cut halfway across the nut.

A] Locking plate

B] Wire lock

C] Self-locking nut

D] Sawn nut

74] Prevents slackening of two bolts.

A] Locking plate

B] Wire lock

C] Self-locking nut

D] Sawn nut

75] Prevents rotation of the top nut.

A] Lock-nut

B] Grooved nut

C] Self-locking nut

D] Sawn nut

76] Prevents loosening of nut by the use of a plate shaped to fit the nut.

A] Locking plate

B] Wire lock

C] Self-locking nut

D] Sawn nut

77] Hexagonal nut with the lower part made cylindrical and the recessed groove.

A] Lock-nut

B] Grooved nut

C] Self-locking nut

D] Sawn nut

78] Drill a blind hole equal to half of the diameter of the stud. Insert this tool into the hole and remove the stud by turning this anticlockwise.

A] Prick Punch Method

B] Filing square very mm

C] Using square taper punch

D] Ezy-out method

79] If the stud is broken near to the surface, employ this method to remove the stud.

A] Prick Punch Method

B] Filing square very mm

C] Using square taper punch

D] Ezy-out method

80] When a stud is broken a little above the surface this method is used to remove the stud.

A] Filing square very mm

B] Using square taper punch

C] Ezy-out method

D] Making drill hole

81] To extract the broken stud a special tool is employed in this method.

A] Prick Punch Method

B] Filing square very mm

C] Using square taper punch

D] Ezy-out method

82] File the protruding stud into square form and remove it.

A] Prick Punch Method

B] Filing square very mm

C] Using square taper punch

D] Ezy-out method

Files

83] The convexity of files helps...

A] To file concave surfaces

B] To file convex surfaces

C] <u>To prevent rounding of edges of work</u>

D] The file to become straight when pressure is applied

84] Which file used for filling wood, leather and other soft material? .

A] Single cut file

B] Double cut file

<u>c] Rasp cut file</u>

D] Curved cut file

85] File used is used for ------------

A] Cleaning the work piece

C] Renewing the file teeth

<u>B] cleaning the file teeth</u>

D] Cleaning the chips

86] File card is used to --------

A] Clean the work piece

C] Renew the file teeth

<u>B] Clean the file teeth</u>

87] Bench grinder are used for ....

A] Heavy duty work

B] Heavy and light duty work

<u>C] Light duty work</u>

D] Lather work

88] Bench Grinders are fitted on a ....

A] Base

<u>B] Table.</u>

C] Wheel guards

D] Conveyor

89] Which one of the following is important factor required to achieve the interchange ability in mass production? .

A] Geometrical accuracy.

B] Standardization

<u>C] Dimensional accuracy</u>

D] Surface finish

90] Interchange ability is normally applied for? _

A] Repairing of parts

<u>B] Mass production</u>

C] Single piece production

D] All of these

91] When tolerance given in one side of the basic dimension, it is called --------

A].Tolerance system

B] Unilateral tolerance

C] Bilateral tolerance

D] Allowance System

92] The measured Size Of the dimensions of a component as called---------

A] Basic size

B] Nominal Size

C] Allowed size

D] Actual size

93] In the drawing the dimensions of a shaft is shown 40i 0068/0042, which is the size of Shaft within the tolerance?

A] 4.0.64 mm

B] 40.042 mm

C] 40.000 mm

D] 39.998 mm

94] In Hole basic system ----------

A] The size of the shaft is made constant

B] The Size of the hole is made constant

C] Only 'allowance is given on the hole

D] The permissible tolerance are given on the hole and the Shaft

95] The Size of a component is given as 24 -0.1. What does -O.1 indicates? _

A] Upper deviation is + 0.1 mm .

B] Lower deviation is 0.0 mm

C] Fundamental deviation is 0.0 mm

D] Lower deviation is _0.1 mm

96] The tolerance of a hole iS the difference between the --

A] Maximum hole Size and maximum Shaft size

B] Maximum hole size and maximum hole Size

C] Minimum 'hole size and maximum Shaft Size

D] Minimum hole Size and minimum shaft Size

97] A hole whose lower deviation is zero is called basic hole. Which one of the following letter indicates basic hole?

A] E

B] F

C] G ‘

<u>D] H</u>

98] Which one having upper deviation zero?

<u>A] Bassc Shaft</u>

B] Basic hole

C] Tolerance

D] Clearance

99] A ball bearing on a shaft is type of fit? ,

A] Clearance fit

<u>B] Driving fit</u>

C] Shrinkage fit

D] None of the above

100] In the BIS system of limits and fits, the grade of tolerance are represented by number Symbols and there are ---------i

A] 14 grades of tolerance

B] 16 grades of tolerance

<u>C] 18 grades of tolerance ’</u>

D] 20 grades of tolerance

Limit fit tolerance

101] A Product is said to have the quality when ....

A] Its shape and dimensions are within the limit

<u>B] It is fit for use</u>

C] It appears to be very good

D] The choice of material is right

102] The maximum clearance required between hole'30 +0.021, 0.000 and shaft 30 -0.110, 0.143 is.

A] 0.110 mm '

B] 0.131 mm

C] 0.164 mm

D] 0.143 mm

103] A dimension is stated as 25 .1002 mm in a drawing. What is the tolerance?

A] +0.02 mm'

B] +0.04 mm

C] -0.02 mm

D] 25.00 mm

104] A pin is fitted in a hole. The tolerance zone of the pin is entirely above that of hole. The fit obtained will be?

A] Clearance fit

B] Transition fit

C] Interference fit

D] Running fit

105] Tolerance is given to the part size to............

A] Production the part within the required permissible size error

B] Increase the production

C] Decrease the Production

D] Finish the components approximately

106] Which one of the following is the clearance fit under the whole basic system?

A] 20 H7/p6'

B] 2067/211

C] ZOG/gll .

D] 20H/g11.

107] The three classes of fits as per BIS system aré ....

A] Clearance fit, interference fit and transition fit

B] Medium fit, push fit and tight fit

C] Flat fit, round fit and square fit

D] 'Sliding fit ', loose fit and shrinkage fit

108] Which one of the following tolerance specifications has a maximum dimensionless than 20 mm?

A] 20 +0.2,-0.3

B] 20 320.2

C] 20 -0.2, 0.3 e

D]m 20 +500, ~03

109] Difference between the maximum and minimum limit is --------------------

A] Single informant

B] Basic shaft

C] Clearance

D] Tolerance

110] A shaft 55 running freely in bush bearing the type of fit is ---------

A] Clearance fit

B] Driving plate

C] shrinkage fit

D] None of the above

111] The taper shank drills are held on the machine by means of...

A] Chucks

B] Sleeves

C] Drift

D] Vice

112] Drill chucks are fitted on the drilling machine spindle by means of a...

A] Knurled ring

B] Arbor

C] Drift

D] Pinion and key

113] The Morse taper provided on drills ranges between...

A] MT 1 to MT 5

B] MT 1 to MT 4

C] MT 0 to MT 5

D] MT 0 to MT 4

114] A drift is used for...

A] Drawing a drill location

B] Fixing chuck on the machine spindle

C] Removing a broken drill from the work

D] Removing the drill from the machine spindle

115] When the taper shank of the drill is larger than the machine spindle, the device to hold the drill is a...

A] Drill sleeve
B] Taper socket
C] Drill drift
D] Chuck and key

116] The suitable cutting fluid for drilling mild steel in a drilling machine is...
A] Synthetic soluble oil
B] Neat oil
C] Distilled water
D] Soluble oil

117] A special feature of the radial drilling machine is...
A] It can be used for drilling with a H.S.S. drill
B] Table can be moved and set at any position
C] A variety of speeds is available
D] The spindle can be brought to any position

118] The point angle of drills depends on...
A] The size of the drill
B] The type of machine
C] The material of the work
D] The RPM of the drill

119] The point angle for a standard drill is...
A] 60◦
B] 108◦
C] 118◦
D] 135◦

120] The helical angle determines the...
A] Cutting angle
B] Chew angle
C] Rake angle
D] Lip angle

121] The clearance angle of the drill is between...
A] 3◦ to 5◦
B] 8◦ to 12◦
C] 12◦ to 20◦
D] 15◦ to 20◦

122] In a remote place (no electricity available] a rail track is to be drilled. Choose the right drilling machine

A] Radial drilling machine

B] Pillar drilling machine

C] Ratchet drilling machine

D] Sensitive drilling Machine

Drilling

123] A drilling machine used by a carpenter for cabinet making is a...

A] Ratchet drilling machine

B] Radial drilling machine

C] Breast drilling machine

D] Sensitive drilling machine

124] Which one of the following drilling machines is used for drilling holes where electricity is not available?

A] Bench drilling machine

B] Pillar drilling machine

C] Redial drilling machine

D] Ratchet drilling machine

125] Which one of the following drilling machine is used for heavy duty work?

A] Bench drilling machine

B] Pillar drilling machine

C] Radial drilling machine

D] Electric hand drilling machine

126] Drill chuck are held on the machine spindle by means of ------

A] arbor

B] Drift

C] draw-in bar

D] Chuck nut

127] Different speeds are obtained in a sensitive bench drilling machine by ----

A] Belt pulley mechanism

B] Hydraulic mechanism

C] Rack and Pinion mechanism

D] Cam and follower mechanism

128] Which one of the following is used only for finishing and maintaining correct form of thread?

A] Tap

B] Threading tool

C] Threading chaser

D] Tipped tool

129] Tap are re-sharpened by grinding ....

A] Flutes

B] Threads

C] Diameter

D] Relief

130] Which size drill is used for taping width MS tap?

A] 4.5 mm

B] 4.0 mm

C] 0.38mm

D] 0.35mm

131] Which one of the following is used to operate form of thread by hand?

A} Tap

B] Threading tool

C] Threading chaser

D] Tipped tool

132] In hand tapping operation, no of taps used are ----

A] 2

B] 3

C] 4

D] 5

133] To get 100% tap in a hole the size of the hole must be equal to ----

A] Minor diameter of the tap

B] Intermediate diameter of the tap

C] Major diameter of the tap

D] None of these

134] A die in which more than one cutting operation is per formed in one stroke

A] Piercing die
B] Progressive die
C] Combination die
D] Compound die

Tap Die

135] A die in which cutting and non cutting operations are carried out per stroke.

A] Piercing die
B] Progressive die
C] Combination die
D] Compound die

136] A die in which two or more sequential operations are performed at two or more stations upon the work.

A] Piercing die
B] Progressive die
C] Combination die
D] Compound die

137] A die in which the shape of the punch and die are directly reproduced in the metal with little or no metal flow.

A] Progressive die
B] Combination die
C] Compound die
D] Forming die

138] The die used for producing any shape of holes.

A] Piercing die
B] Progressive die
C] Combination die
D] Compound die

139] A short reamer with an axial hole used with an arbor or mandrel is called -------

A] Parallel reamer

B] Adjustable reamer

C] Expansion reamer

D] Chucking reamer

Reamer

140] Which one of the following machine reamers is used to correct the misalignment between the reamer axis and the work axis?

A] Floating blade reamer

B] Machine jig reamer.

C] Shell reamer

D] Chucking reamer

141] for making gutters, roof flashing, hoods etc.

A] Galvanised iron

B] Stainless steel

C] Copper sheet

D] Metal sheets

142] in dairies. food processing, kitchen ware etc.

A] Galvanised iron

B] Stainless steel

C] Copper sheet

D] Metal sheets

143] for making buckets, heating ducts, cabinets etc.

A] Galvanised iron

B] Stainless steel

C] Copper sheet

D] Metal sheets

144] in canneries and chemical plants Metal sheets

A] Galvanised iron
B] Stainless steel
C] Copper sheet
D] Metal sheets
145] Ammonium chloride is used as a flux for soldering...
A] steel
B] aluminium
C] galvanized iron
D] stainless steel
146] Soldering of M.S sheets takes place at a temperature of...
A] 150°C
B] 250°C
C] 400°C
D] 850°C
147.] In soldering operation the base metal is...
A.] not heated
B.] heated to 200°C
C.] heated to 650°C
D.] heated to red hot condition
148] Rivets for Joining sheets to thick plates.
A] Countersunk head
B] Flat head
C] Pan head
D] Mushroom
149] Rivets for Joining sheet metal.
A] Countersunk head
B] Flat head
C] Pan head
D] Mushroom
150] Rivets for Heavy fabrication work.
A] Countersunk head
B] Flat head
C] Pan head
D] Mushroom
151] Rivets for Reduces the height of rivet head above the meta\ surface
A] Countersunk head
B] Flat head

C] Pan head

D] Mushroom

152] Rivets for commonly used for structural work.

A] Countersunk head

B] Flat head

C] Pan head

D] Snap head

153.] The alternator in a car delivers 4A and has a load of 3 ohms connected across its terminals. Find the voltage of the circuit

A] 18V

B] 24V

C] 12V

D] 16V

Dynamo (Alternator) distributor cap in car

154] A voltage source produces an IR drop of 40V across a 20 ohms resistance, 60V across a 30 ohms resistance and 180V across a 90 ohms resistance all in series. How much is the applied voltage?

A] 180 V

B] 240 V

C] 100 V

D] 280 V

155] How big is the peak amplitude of a sine-wave with an effective value of 220 volts?

A] 311 V

B] 380 V

C] 400 V

D] 440 V

156] The peak-to-peak voltage is 99V. how big is the effective value of the sine wave?

A] 70 V

B] 44.5V

C] 49.5 V

D] 35 V

157] A moving coil voltmeter reads 10 V AC. How big is the effective voltage?

A] higher

B] lower

C] the same

D] 10% higher

158] A moving iron ammeter reads 10 A. how big is the peak current of the oscillation?

A] 7.07 A

B] 1.1414A

C] 70.7 A

D] 14.1 A

159] A current of 2 amps flows through a resistance of 10 ohms. The power dissipated in the resistance is equal to...

A. 20 watts

B. 200 watts

C. 40 watts

D. 5 watts

160] Power companies are interested in improving the power factor to

A] reduce line current

B] increase motor efficiency

C] increase volt-amperes

D] decrease power

161.] Moving coil instrument works on the effect of...

A] chemical effect

B] heating effect

C] electrostatic effect

D] electromagnetic effect

162] The angle of below pipe to the line of weld in leftward welding technique is...

A] 40 to 50◦

B] 50 to 60◦

C] 60 to 70◦

D. 70 to 80◦

163] The angle of filler rod in case of rightward welding technique is...

A] 10 to 20◦

B] 20 to 30◦

C] 30 to 40◦

D] 40 to 50◦

164] Forge welding is classified as...

A] Fusion welding without pressure

B] Fusion welding with pressure

C] Non-fusion welding without pressure

D] no-fusion welding with pressure

165] One of the functions of flux in gas welding is...

A] Dissolve the metal oxides

B] Reduce the melting point of mental

C] Increase the flame temperature

D] Increase the root penetration

166] On which of the following factors, the choice of flux for gas welding depend?

A] type of material to be joined

B] type of edge penetration

C] type of fuel gas

D] type of flame used

167] Shielded metal arc welding is classified under the process of...

A] Electric resistance welding

B] Special welding

C] Electric arc welding

D] Electro gas welding

168] How to specify the size of an electrode holder?

A] By its weight

B] By its shape

C] By its current carrying capacity

D] By the metal used for making it

169] Which metal pipe should NOT be used for passing acetylene gas in order to avoid explosions?

A] Galvanized iron

B] Stainless steel

C] Mild steel

D] Cooper

170] He percentage of carbon in acetylene gas is...

A] 99%

B] 92.3%

C] 89.1%

D] 85.3%

171] Acetylene gas contains

A] Calcium, carbon and hydrogen

B] Calcium and hydrogen

C] Calcium, carbon, hydrogen and oxygen

D] Carbon and hydrogen

172] In an acetylene purifier the sulphureted and phosphorated hydrogen are removed by...

A] Pumice

B] Water

C] Filter wool

D] Purifying chemicals

173] Maximum temperature for forging H. S. S. is -------------degree.

A] 1200

B] 100

C] 1100

D] 1500

174] Main purpose Of annealing is -----------.

A] To improve machinability

B] To improve magnetism

C] To increase hardness

D] To increase toughness

175] The carbon percentage in H.S.S. tool is -------

A] 0.75 to 1.00 %

B] 1.00 to 2.00 00

C] 0.60 to 0.75 %

D] 0.02 to 0.03 %.

176] Which one of the following is the resistance of a metal to elastic deformation?

A] Ductility.

B] Strength

C] Stiffness

D] Toughness

177] The process of heating and cooling to change the structure of steel for obtaining the required properties is called

A] Hardening

B] Normalizing

C] Heat treatment

D] Tempering

178] The main purpose of annealing is to

A] Increase the hardness

B] Increase the toughness

C] Improve machinability

D] Improve distortion

179] The purpose of normalizing steel is to -----------

A] Remove the induced Stress

B] Improve genes and reduce brittleness

C] Soften the metal

D] Increase the surface?

180] Which one of the following process is used for hardenmg the outer 5" Annealing

A] Hardening

B] Tempering

C] Case Hardening

D] Tear surface

181] The purpose of producmg a component with tough and ductIle core and hard ou is known as......

A] Hardening

B] Case hardening

C] Tempering

D] Annealing

182] Lower critical temperature of high carbon steel while hardening is ----------

A] 9600C

B] 900°C

c] 7230 c

D] 56O C

183] The process of Changing the structure and thus changing the properties by heating and 'cooling is known as --

A] Heat treatment

B] Alloying

C] Tempering

D] None of these

184] For refining the grain structure which one of the following heat treatment processes 'Is adopted.

A] Annealing

B] Hardening

C] Tempering

D] Normalising

185] Annealing is performed on iron and steel ---------

A] To remove internal stresses

B] To reduce hardness

C] To improve machinability

D] All of these

186] Which one of the following does not fall under the stages of heat treatment?

A] Heating

B] Cleaning

C] Quenching

D] Soaking

187] Fluid under pressures

A] To start heavy duty engine

B] Starter motor

C] Hydraulic cranking

D] Electric motor

188] Gasoline engine

A] To start heavy duty engine

B] Starter motor

C] Hydraulic cranking

D] Electric motor

189] Battery power

A] To start heavy duty engine

B] Starter motor

C] Hydraulic cranking

D] Electric motor

Starter winding armature in vehicle

190] Air compressor's driven by
A] To start heavy duty engine
B] Starter motor
C] Hydraulic cranking
D] <u>Electric motor</u>
191] Hydraulic floor jack is used
A] To remove king pin bush
B] <u>To lift the wheel</u>
C] To press the bush
D] Hold the job.
192] The most popular chuck on surface grinder is ----------
A] Pneumatic chuck
B] Hydraulic chuck
<u>C] Magnetic chuck</u>
D] Three law chuck
193] Which one of the following is the advantage of pneumatic system?
A] For low cost layout
B] For increasing the rate of production
C] For better working environment
<u>D] All of these</u>
194] Allows fluid both way in and out of cylinder
A] Piston
B] Push Rod
C] Primary cup
D] <u>Check valve</u>
195] Relieves excess pressure of air from the air tank.
A] Air compressor
B] Unloader valve
C] <u>Safety valve</u>
D] Brake chamber

Air tank safety valve

196] Regulates maximum air pressure, reaching to air tank.
A] Air compressor
B] Unloader valve
C] Safety valve
D] Brake chamber

Brakes in car

197] Supplies air to front and rear brake
A] Brake actuator
B] Dual brake valve
C] System protection valve
D] Flick valve
198] Operated for parking the vehicle.
A] Brake actuator
B] Dual brake valve
C] System protection valve
D] Flick valve
199] Distributes air to various circuits
A] Brake actuator
B] Dual brake valve
C] System protection valve
200] Keeps valves in closed position
A] Push Rod
B] Tappet
C] Spring
D] Cam lobe

Engine valves

201] Allow fuel to flow in and out

A] Valves

B] Coil spring

C] Diaphragm

D] Rocker arm

Cooling system in car

202] Allows coolants into the expansion tank

A] Pressure relief valve

B] Engine fan belt

C] Radiator drain plug

D] Over flow pipe

203] An overflow valve is used

A] to send back excess fuel from the fuel filler

B] to supply more fuel to the fuel filter

C] to supply clean fuel

D] to take the leaking fuel.

204] Provides compressed air to system

A] Air compressor

B] Unloader valve

C] Safety valve

D] Brake chamber

205] Air compressor's driven by

A] To start heavy duty engine

B] Starter motor
C] Hydraulic cranking
D] Electric motor
206] Air compressors is used for
A] Multipurpose
B] To lift the car only
C] To lift and remove the wheel
D] To grind the chisel.
207] in the air compressor, the safety device is used to
A] To suck the air
B] To release the air completely
C] To regulate the air pressure
D] To release excess air pressure.
208] Used in air compressor
A] Pressure gauge
B] Oil tank
C] Oil spray gun
D] Car hoist
209] Increases road wheel torque
A] Engine
B] Clutches
C] Final drive
D] U joints
210] Helps to turn the stub axles
A] Front axle
B] Track rod
C] Stub axle
D] Stub axle arm
211] Carries springs and steering linkages.
A] Front axle
B] Track rod
C] Stub axle
D] Stub axle arm

Steering gearbox in vehicle

212] Transmits steering wheel movement to stub axle
A] Front axle
B] Track rod
C] Stub axle
D] Stub axle arm

213] Pivots about king pin for steering purpose
A] Front axle
B] Track rod
C] Stub axle
D] Stub axle arm

214] Fuel catching fire
A] T.D.C.
B] Cycle
C] B.D.C.
D] Ignition

215] To seal the tank externally.
A] Baffles
B] Filter cap
C] Passage in the baffle
D] Filler neck

216] Prevents slashing of fuel in the tank
A] Baffles
B] Filter cap
C] Passage in the baffle
D] Filler neck

217] To fill fuel in the tank

A] Baffles
B] Filter cap
C] Passage in the baffle
D] Filler neck
218] To transfer fuel from one compartment to other compartment
A] Baffles
B] Filter cap
C] Passage in the baffle
D] Filler neck
219] Carries fuel
A] Carburettor
B] Pump
C] Pipe lines
D] Petrol tank
220] Stores petrol
A] Carburettor
B] Pump
C] Pipe lines
D] Petrol tank
221] Delivers petrol to the engine
A] Carburettor
B] Pump
C] Pipe lines
D] Petrol tank
222] Delivers petrol to carburettor
A] Carburettor
B] Pump
C] Pipe lines
D] Petrol tank

Fuel pump in Vehicle

223] Holds petrol

A] Air horn

B] Fuel bowl

C] Air cleaner

D] Air bleed

224] Serves as passage for air

A] Air horn

B] Fuel bowl

C] Air cleaner

D] Air bleed

225] Helps in breaking up fuel particles

A] Air horn

B] Fuel bowl

C] Air cleaner

D] Air bleed

226] Develops pressure on fuel to go out

A] Valves
B] Coil spring
C] <u>Diaphragm</u>
D] Rocker arm
227] Used to lift the vehicle
A] Pressure gauge
B] Oil tank
C] Oil spray gun
D] <u>Car hoist</u>
228] Used in car hoist
A] Pressure gauge
B] <u>Oil tank</u>
C] Oil spray gun
D] Car hoist
229] In diesel cycle Combustion takes place at
A] <u>Constant pressure</u>
B] Constant volume' '
C] Constant temperature
D] Constant temperature and pressure.
230] Rudolf Diesel, developed a Cl.engine
A] 1876
B] 1880
C] <u>1892</u>
D] 1930

231] Perkins built ‘P‘ series engines
A] 1876
B] 1880
C] 1892
D] 1930
232] N.A OTTO developed a 4 stroke cycle engine
A] 1876
B] 1880
C] 1892
D] 1930
233] Dugald Clerk developed a 2 stroke cycle engine
A] 1876
B] 1880
C] 1892
D] 1930
234] All cylinders in a horizontal line
A] ‘V’ Engine
B] Inline Engine
C] Opposed Engine
D] Radial Engine
235] Cylinders positioned in ‘V‘ shape
A] ‘V‘ Engine
B] Inline Engine
C] Opposed Engine
D] Radial Engine
236] Cylinders positioned radially
A] ‘V’ Engine
B] Inline Engine
C] Opposed Engine
D] Radial Engine
237] Cylinders arranged horizontally opposite to each other
A] ‘V‘ Engine
B] Inline Engine
C] Opposed Engine
D] Radial Engine
238] Indicate rate of battery charging current
A] Ammeter
B] Speedometer

C] Clutch pedal
D] Ignition switch
239] indicates the speed in Km/Hr
A] Ammeter
B] Speedometer
C] Clutch pedal
D] Ignition switch
240] Allow to flow the current in starting circuit in engine
A] Ammeter
B] Speedometer
C] Clutch pedal
D] Ignition switch
241] What IS the reason for hissing noise from cylinder head?
A] excessive tappet clearance
B] wrong injection timing
C] pie-ignition
D] air cleaner mounting loose.
242] Mounted on cylinder head or block
A] Fins
B] Radiators
C] Fan
D] Water pump
243] Which component among the following reduces noise of exhaust gases?
A] Exhaust pipe
B] Muffler
C] inlet manifold
D] tail pipe.
244] Specific gravity of battery electrolyte is checked by
A] ammeter
B] Voltmeter
C] Hydrometer
D] Tachometer.

Lead acid battery in vehicle

245] Oil level is checked by
A] Dip stick
B] Ammeter
C] Oil pressure gauge
D] Fuel gauge.

246] Used as parking light Cum indicator
A] A symmetrical bulb
B] Miniature bulb
C] Festoon bulb
D] S.C./ S.F.

247] Used as no plate lamp and brake lamp
B] Miniature bulb
C] Festoon bulb
D] S.C / S.F.
E] D.C/ D.F.

248] Used as two wheeler tail lamp
A] A symmetrical bulb
B] Miniature bulb
C] Festoon bulb
D] S.C/ S.F.

249] Used as panel instrument lamp
A] A symmetrical bulb
B] Miniature bulb
C] Festoon bulb
D] S.C.IS.F.

250] Used as headlight bulb

A] A symmetrical bulb
B] Miniature bulb
C] Festoon bulb
D] S.C.IS.F.
251] The head light parts can be replaced in
A] sealed beam
B] flush fitting type
C] prefocused bulb
D] halogen bulbs.
252] The head light is also used as
A] Side indicator
B] Stop indicator
C] Signalling device
D] Heating device.
253] To direct the shell light rays onto the road
A] Headlamp
B] Reflector
C] Lens
D] Adopter
254] To hold the bulb in the holder
A] Headlamp
B] Reflector
C] Lens
D] Adopter
255] To produce illumination
B] Reflector
C] Lens
D] Adopter
E] Bulb
256] To produce flat oval shaped beam
A] Headlamp
B] Reflector
C] Lens
D] Adopter
257] To hold the reflector in position
A] Headlamp
B] Reflector
C] Lens

D] Adopter
258] To indicate the vehicle is being braked
A] Headlight
B] Parking light
C] Stop light
D] Panel light
259] To read the working of gauges
A] Headlight
B] Parking light
C] Stop light
D] Panel light
260] To provide illumination on the road
A] Headlight
B] Parking light
C] Stop light
D] Panel light
261] to indicate the parking ' of vehicle
A] Headlight
B] Parking light
C] Stop light
D] Panel light
262] Feed pumps are driven by
A] camshaft of engine
B] Camshaft of FIP
C] Timing Gears
D] Varies from engine to engine.
263] The oil pumps are generally driven by
A] camshaft
B] rocker shaft
C] crankshaft
D] damper pulley
264]Engine develops less power due to
A]defective ignition timing
B]excessive rich mixture
C]defective lubrication system
D]too tight cylinder head
265] Supplies fluid to front and rear wheels
A] Brake pedal

B] Master cylinder piston
C] Wheel cylinder piston
D] <u>Distribution block</u>
266] Pushes the brake shoe towards drum
A] Brake pedal
B] Master cylinder piston
C] <u>Wheel cylinder piston</u>
D] Distribution block

Piston & rings in Engine

267] Creates pressure on fluid
A] Brake pedal
B] <u>Master cylinder piston</u>
C] Wheel cylinder piston
D] Distribution block
268] Pushes master cylinder piston through linkages.
A] <u>Brake pedal</u>
B] Master cylinder piston
C] Wheel cylinder piston
D] Distribution block
269] Allows fluid both way in and out of cylinder
A] Piston
B] Push Rod
C] Primary cup
D] <u>Check valve</u>
270] Seals the compensating port

A] Piston
B] Push Rod
C] Primary cup
D] Check valve
271] Actuates the piston
A] Piston
B] Push Rod
C] Primary cup
D] Check valve
272] Develops pressure on fluid
A] Piston
B] Push Rod
C] Primary cup
D] Check valve
273] Displacement volume of piston
A] I.H.P.
B] Swept volume
C] Mechanical efficiency
D] Horse power
274] Starting point of piston's downward movement in the cylinder
A] T.D.C.
B] Cycle
C] B.D.C.
D] Ignition
275] Starting point of piston's upward movement in the cylinder
A] T.D.C.
B] Cycle
C] B.D.C.
D] Ignition
276] Prevents blow by
A] Piston
B] Piston pin
C] Connecting rod
D] Piston rings
277] Reciprocates in the cylinder
A] Piston
B] Piston pin
C] Connecting rod

D] Piston rings

278] Connects piston and connecting rod

A] Piston

B] Piston pin

C] Connecting rod

D] Piston rings

279] Oscillates in cylinder

A] Piston

B] Piston pin

C] Connecting rod

D] Piston rings

280]The top and bottom halves of connecting rod are bolted on

A] crankshaft man journal

B] crankpin journal

C] camshaft

D] piston pin boss

281] A hole is drilled between crankshaft main journal and crank pin for

A] balancing of crankshaft

B] reducing crankshaft weight

C] lubricating connecting rod bearings

D] reducing crankshaft vibrations

282] Converts reciprocating motion into rotary motion

A] Crankshaft

B] Flywheels

C] Torque wrench

D] Thrust bearing

283] Rotary movement to pull and push action

A] Wiper motor

B] Cranking link

C] Pinion

D] Wiper blade

284] Accommodates wheel hub bearings.

A] Kingpin

B] Spring pad

C] Stub axle shaft portion

D] Track rod ball joints

285] Pushes with drawal plate

A] Clutch cover

B] Release bearing
C] Release fingers
D] Clutch plate
286] Takes thrust load
A] Crankshaft
B] Flywheels
C] Torque wrench
D] Thrust bearing
287]Distributor shaft is supported by
A] ball bearing
B] shell bearing
C] bush bearing
D] needle bearing
288] Stores energy
A] Crankshaft
B] Flywheels
C] Torque wrench
D] Thrust bearing
289] engages with the flywheel ring
A] Pinion
B] Over running clutch
C] Plunger disk
D] Clutch
290] Flywheel magneto consists of
A] Temporary magnet
B] Bar magnet
C] Permanent magnet
D] Needle magnet.
291] in flywheel magneto, the ignition coil is
A] stationary
B] Moving
C] Rotating
D] Oscillating.
292] To rotate the permanent magnet
A] Switch
B] Secondary coils
C] Flywheels
D] Condensers

293]The boiling temperature of the coolant in the cooling in the cooling system is increased by the use of

A]water jackets

B]vacuum valve only

C]pressure type radiator cap

D] radiator core tubes/pipes

Radiator cap in vehicle

294] The main purpose of pressure radiator cap is to

A]pressurize the system

B]increase air water circulation

C]help to develop vacuum in the system

D]avoid build up to pressure

295] one of the following causes may also contribute to overheating of an engine

A]clogged radiator cores

B]low idle speed setting

C]excessive valve tappet clearance

D]lubricating oil pressure is too high

296] Mounted on cylinder head or block

A] Fins

B] Radiators

C] Fan

D] Water pump

297] Drives the water pump

A] Pressure relief valve

B] Engine fan belt

C] Radiator drain plug

D] Over flow pipe

Thermostat valve in vehicle

298] If thermostat valve remains in an open position then which of the following will happen

A]slow warming up to engine

B]engine will over heat

C]engine fails to start

D]stalling of engine

299]In a dry sump lubrication system, a scavenging pump is used to

A] pump oil from sump to tank

B] pump oil directly to all moving parts

C] develop additional oil pressure

D] pump oil from tank to sum

300]Excessive oil pressure in the lubrication system may be due to

A] less quantity of engine oil in sump

B] incorrect adjustment of relief valve

C] less suction effect on the suction pipe

D] none of the above

301] when oil pressure increases above set limit, oil returns to sump through

A]pressure relief valve

B]by pass valve

C]oil filter

D]oil pump

302] low engine oil pressure may be due to

A]clogged oil filter

B]more oil filled in the oil sump

C]high viscosity of oil used

D]excessive backlash between pump gears

303] Cleans the air entering the cylinder

A] Air horn

B] Fuel bowl

C] Air cleaner

D] Air bleed

304] connect two terminals of solenoid.

A] Pinion

B] Over running clutch

C] Plunger disk

D] Clutch

305] When the horn button is pressed the current flows to horn through

A] Horn switch

B] Solenoid coil

C] Battery

D] Chassis.

306] Turns core to magnet

A] Solenoid Switch

B] Actuating wire (when heated]

C] Ballast Resistors

D] Actuating wire (when cooled]

307] What IS the reason for hissing noise from cylinder head?

A] excessive tappet clearance

B] wrong injection timing

C] pie-ignition

D] air cleaner mounting loose.

INDUSTRIAL TRAINING INSTITUTE

Monthly Test-1, Marks- 20, Date:- ______________

(Every Question Carry Two Marks)

1-06] Benefit of SS system is ------

A] Increase in productivity

B] Increase in quality

C] Reduction in wastage of time

D] All of these

2-07] Safety is -----------

A] Nobody's business

B] Every bodies business

C] Some bodies business

D] The organization business

3-08] For basic categories of safety signs are available The meaning of "prohibition" sign ----

A] Shows it must not be done

B] Shows what must be done

C] Warns the hazard or danger

D] Gives information of safety provision

4-09] Which one is a workshop safety?

A] Keep shop floor clean and free from grease, oil or other slippery materials

B] Stop the machine before changing the speed

C] Don't use cracked or chipped tools

D] Don't try to stop a running machine with hand

5-10] In Personal Protect Equipment (PPE] HELMET is used to

A] Protect head

B] Protect eyes

C] Protect hands

D] Protect ears

6-11] Which of the following belongs to general safety?

A Have a worker in good attitude

B] The work clean and clear

C] Concentrate on your work

D] Keep the floor and gangways clean and clear

7-12] While grinding, which is used to protect the eyes?

A] Dark green glass

B] Mask

C] Sun glasses

D] Safety goggles

8-13] Which of the following is done for machine safety?

A] Check the oil level before starting the machine

B] Do things in a methodical way

C] Keep the floor and gangways clean and clear

D] Don't use dies and scarves

9-14] In Personal Protect Equipment (PPE], 'sleeves' is used to protect ----------

A] Face

B] Eyes

C] Ears

D] Hands

10-15] ABC stands for -------------

A] Automatic Breathing Control

B] Automatic Blood Control

C] Airway Breathing Circulation

D] Automatic Blood Circulation

INDUSTRIAL TRAINING INSTITUTE

Monthly Test-2, Marks- 20, Date:- ______________

(Every Question Carry Two Marks)

1-21] The instrument used to mark parallel lines, parallel to the datum edge is -

A] Jenny caliper

B] Divider

C] Outside calliper

D] Inside calliper

2-22] Which one of the following is an indirect measuring tool?

A] Outside caliper

B] Vernier calliper

C] Steel rule

D] Outside micrometer

3-23] For cutting thin tubing, the most suitable pitch of the hacksaw blade is...

A] 1.8mm

B] 1.4mm

C] 1mm

D] 0.8mm

4-24] For cutting solid brass, the most suitable pitch of the hacksaw blade is...

A] 1.8mm

B] 1.4mm

C] 1mm

D] 0.8mm

5-25] A new hacksaw blade after a few strokes becomes loose because of the...

A] Stretching of the blade

B] Wing-nut threads being worn out

C] Wrong pitch of the blade

D] Improper selection of the set of saws.

6-26] While cutting small diameter pipes, it is advisable to watch regularly and ensure that...

A] The cut is along the curved line

B] More saw teeth are in contract

C] The work is not overheated

D] Proper balancing of hacksaw is maintained

7-27] The vice clamps are used to...

A] Protect hard jaws

B] Clamp the work pieces rigidly

C] Protect the finished surfaces

D] Prevent the movable jaw being filed

8-28] The reference surface during marking is provided by the...

A] Surface gauge

B] Work piece

C] Drawing of the work

D] Marking table surface

9-29] The size of an engineer's vice is specified by the...

A] Length of the movable jaw

B] Width of the jaws

C] Height of the vice

D] Maximum opening of the jaws

10-30] Portion of the hammer used for fixing the handle is...

A] Face

B] Peen

C] Cheek

D] Eye hole

INDUSTRIAL TRAINING INSTITUTE

Monthly Test-3, Marks- 20, Date:- _______________

(Every Question Carry Two Marks)

1-36] Name the punch used to locate the centre.

A] Prick punch 30°

B] Prick punch 60°

C] Centre punch

D] Dot punch

2-37] The point angle of centre punch is --------

A] 30°

B] 50°

c] 900

D] 1200

3-38] Punches are used for forming ---------of any shape

A] Holes

B] Mining

C] Knurling

D] Reaming

4-39] Generally the length of the handle of the vice is ----------

A] 1.5 times the normal size of the vice

B] 2.5 times the normal size of the vice

C] 3.5 times the normal size of the vice

D] 4.5 times the normal size of the vice

5-40] Bench vice spindle is made of ....

A] Mild steel

B] Cast iron

C] Tool steel

D] Bronze

6-41] The part of the universal surface gauge which helps to draw a parallel line along a datum edge is the..

A] Rocker arm

B] Snug

C] Fine adjustment screw

D] Guide pins

7-42] Scribers are made of...

A] Mild steel

B] High carbon steel
C] Brass
D. Cast iron
8-43] The point angle of scriber is -----------
A] 30°
B] 60°
C] 5° to 10°
D] 12° to 15°
9-44] The cutting angle for chipping cast iron is...
A] 37.5?
B] 55?
C] 60?
D] 90?
10-45] The chisel will dig into the material when...
A] The rake angle is more
B] The clearance angle is too low
C] The angle of inclination is more
D] The angle of inclination is too low

INDUSTRIAL TRAINING INSTITUTE

Monthly Test-4, Marks- 20, Date:- ______________

(Every Question Carry Two Marks)

1-51] in a metric micrometer, a complete revolution of thimble advances -----------
A] 0.01 mm
B] 0.25 mm
C] 0.50 mm
D] 1.00mm
2-52] Ratchet Stop in the micrometer helps to ------------
A] Control the pressure
B] Lock the spindle
C] Adjust the zero error
D] Hold the work piece
3-53] 1000 micron means ------------
A] 1 mm
B] 1 m
C] 1000 mm
D] 10 cm
4-54] What is the zero reading of a 50-75 mm outside micrometer?

A] 0.000 mm
B] 0.01 mm
C] 25.00 mm
D] 50.00 mm

5-55] The value of the smallest division on sleeve of a metric outside micrometer is -----

A] 0.50 mm
B] 1.00 mm
C] 1.50 mm
D] 2.00 mm

6-56] Ratchet stop in the micrometer helps to ---------

A] Control the pressure
B] Lock the spindle
C] Adjust the zero error
D] Hold the work piece

7-57] Least count of depth micrometer is

A] 0.5 mm
B] 0.2 mm
C] 0.001 mm
D] 0.01 mm

8-58] The least count of vernier calliper is (main scale = 49 division, vernier scale = 50 division]

A] 0.1 mm
B] 0.01 mm
C] 0.001 mm
D] 0.02 mm

9-59] The type of measurement made by using a Vernier Calliper is -------

A] Direct measurement
B] Indirect measurement
C] 90“] (a] 81 (b]
D] None of these

10-60] Telescopic gauges are used to measure holes and slots.

A] from 10 mm to 100 mm
B] from 12 mm to 152 mm
C] from 12.7 mm to 152.4 mm
D] none of the above

Monthly Test-5, Marks- 20, Date:- ______________

(Every Question Carry Two Marks)

1-66] Threading tools are checked for accuracy for the 60? angle by using a

A] Thread plug gauge

B] centre gauge

C] screw pitch gauge

D] tool angle gauge

2-67] The number of threads per inch can be checked with a

A] tool gauge

B] metric rule by counting

C] ring gauge

D] screw pitch gauge

3-68] Used where bolt and threads are to be protected from damage.

A] Donald cap nut

B] Thumb nut

C] Hexagonal nut

D] Wing-nut

4-69] Used where frequent removal and fixing is required.

A] Donald cap nut

B] Thumb nut

C] Hexagonal nut

D] Wing-nut

5-70] Used in machine building and structure work.

A] Donald cap nut

B] Thumb nut

C] Hexagonal nut

D] Wing-nut

6-71] Used where frequent adjustments are to be made.

A] Donald cap nut

B] Thumb nut

C] Hexagonal nut

D] Wing-nut

7-72] Nylon inserts in the nut prevent loosening.

A] Locking plate

B] Wire lock

C] Self-locking nut

D] Sawn nut

8-73] A slot is cut halfway across the nut.

A] Locking plate

B] Wire lock

C] Self-locking nut

D] Sawn nut

9-74] Prevents slackening of two bolts.

A] Locking plate

B] Wire lock

C] Self-locking nut

D] Sawn nut

10-75] Prevents rotation of the top nut.

A] Lock-nut

B] Grooved nut

C] Self-locking nut

D] Sawn nut

INDUSTRIAL TRAINING INSTITUTE

Monthly Test-6, Marks- 20, Date:- _______________

(Every Question Carry Two Marks)

1-81] To extract the broken stud a special tool is employed in this method.

A] Prick Punch Method

B] Filing square very mm

C] Using square taper punch

D] Ezy-out method

2-82] File the protruding stud into square form and remove it.

A] Prick Punch Method

B] Filing square very mm

C] Using square taper punch

D] Ezy-out method

3-83] The convexity of files helps...

A] To file concave surfaces

B] To file convex surfaces

C] To prevent rounding of edges of work

D] The file to become straight when pressure is applied

4-84] Which file used for filling wood, leather and other soft material? .

A] Single cut file

B] Double cut file

c] Rasp cut file

D] Curved cut file

5-85] File used is used for ------------

A] Cleaning the work piece

C] Renewing the file teeth

B] cleaning the file teeth

D] Cleaning the chips

6-86] File card is used to --------

A] Clean the work piece

C] Renew the file teeth

B] Clean the file teeth

7-87] Bench grinder are used for ....

A] Heavy duty work

B] Heavy and light duty work

C] Light duty work

D] Lather work

8-88] Bench Grinders are fitted on a ....

A] Base

B] Table.

C] Wheel guards

D] Conveyor

9-89] Which one of the following is important factor required to achieve the interchange ability in mass production? .

A] Geometrical accuracy.

B] Standardization

C] Dimensional accuracy

D] Surface finish

10-90] Interchange ability is normally applied for? _

A] Repairing of parts

B] Mass production

C] Single piece production

D] All of these

INDUSTRIAL TRAINING INSTITUTE

Monthly Test-7, Marks- 20, Date:- _______________

(Every Question Carry Two Marks)

1-96] The tolerance of a hole iS the difference between the --

A] Maximum hole Size and maximum Shaft size

B] Maximum hole size and maximum hole Size

C] Minimum 'hole size and maximum Shaft Size

D] Minimum hole Size and minimum shaft Size

2-97] A hole whose lower deviation is zero is called basic hole. Which one of the following letter indicates basic hole?

A] E

B] F

C] G ‘

D] H

3-98] Which one having upper deviation zero?

A] Bassc Shaft

B] Basic hole

C] Tolerance

D] Clearance

4-99] A ball bearing on a shaft is type of fit? ,

A] Clearance fit

B] Driving fit

C] Shrinkage fit

D] None of the above

5-100] In the BIS system of limits and fits, the grade of tolerance are represented by number Symbols and there are ---------i

A] 14 grades of tolerance

B] 16 grades of tolerance

C] 18 grades of tolerance ’

D] 20 grades of tolerance

6-101] A Product is said to have the quality when ....

A] Its shape and dimensions are within the limit

B] It is fit for use

C] It appears to be very good

D] The choice of material is right

7-102] The maximum clearance required between hole‘30 +0.021, 0.000 and shaft 30 -0.110, 0.143 is.

A] 0.110 mm ’

B] 0.131 mm

C] 0.164 mm

D] 0.143 mm

8-103] A dimension is stated as 25 .1002 mm in a drawing. What is the tolerance?

A] +0.02 mm'

B] +0.04 mm

C] -0.02 mm

D] 25.00 mm

9-104] A pin is fitted in a hole. The tolerance zone of the pin is entirely above that of hole. The fit obtained will be?

A] Clearance fit

B] Transition fit

C] Interference fit

D] Running fit

10-105] Tolerance is given to the part size to...........

A] Production the part within the required permissible size error

B] Increase the production

C] Decrease the Production

D] Finish the components approximately

INDUSTRIAL TRAINING INSTITUTE

Monthly Test-8, Marks- 20, Date:- _______________

(Every Question Carry Two Marks)

1-111] The taper shank drills are held on the machine by means of...

A] Chucks

B] Sleeves

C] Drift

D] Vice

2-112] Drill chucks are fitted on the drilling machine spindle by means of a...

A] Knurled ring

B] Arbor

C] Drift

D] Pinion and key

3-113] The Morse taper provided on drills ranges between...

A] MT 1 to MT 5

B] MT 1 to MT 4

C] MT 0 to MT 5

D] MT 0 to MT 4

4-114] A drift is used for...

A] Drawing a drill location

B] Fixing chuck on the machine spindle

C] Removing a broken drill from the work

D] Removing the drill from the machine spindle

5-115] When the taper shank of the drill is larger than the machine spindle, the device to hold the drill is a...

A] Drill sleeve

B] Taper socket

C] Drill drift

D] Chuck and key

6-116] The suitable cutting fluid for drilling mild steel in a drilling machine is...

A] Synthetic soluble oil

B] Neat oil

C] Distilled water

D] Soluble oil

7-117] A special feature of the radial drilling machine is...

A] It can be used for drilling with a H.S.S. drill

B] Table can be moved and set at any position

C] A variety of speeds is available

D] The spindle can be brought to any position

8-118] The point angle of drills depends on...

A] The size of the drill

B] The type of machine

C] The material of the work

D] The RPM of the drill

9-119] The point angle for a standard drill is...

A] 60?

B] 108?

C] 118?

D] 135?

10-120] The helical angle determines the...

A] Cutting angle

B] Chew angle

C] Rake angle

D] Lip angle

INDUSTRIAL TRAINING INSTITUTE

Monthly Test-9, Marks- 20, Date:- _______________

(Every Question Carry Two Marks)

1-126] Drill chuck are held on the machine spindle by means of ------

A] arbor

B] Drift

C] draw-in bar

D] Chuck nut

2-127] Different speeds are obtained in a sensitive bench drilling machine by ----

A] Belt pulley mechanism

B] Hydraulic mechanism

C] Rack and Pinion mechanism

D] Cam and follower mechanism

3-128] Which one of the following is used only for finishing and maintaining correct form of thread?

A] Tap

B] Threading tool

C] Threading chaser

D] Tipped tool

4-129] Tap are re-sharpened by grinding ....

A] Flutes

B] Threads

C] Diameter

D] Relief

5-130] Which size drill is used for taping width MS tap?

A] 4.5 mm

B] 4.0 mm

C] 0.38mm

D] 0.35mm

6-131] Which one of the following is used to operate form of thread by hand?

A} Tap

B] Threading tool

C] Threading chaser

D] Tipped tool

7-132] In hand tapping operation, no of taps used are ----

A] 2

B] 3

C] 4

D] 5

8-133] To get 100% tap in a hole the size of the hole must be equal to ----

A] Minor diameter of the tap

B] Intermediate diameter of the tap

C] Major diameter of the tap

D] None of these

9-134] A die in which more than one cutting operation is per formed in one stroke

A] Piercing die

B] Progressive die

C] Combination die

D] Compound die

10-135] A die in which cutting and non cutting operations are carried out per stroke.

A] Piercing die

B] Progressive die

C] Combination die

D] Compound die

INDUSTRIAL TRAINING INSTITUTE

Monthly Test-10, Marks- 20, Date:- ______________

(Every Question Carry Two Marks)

1-141] for making gutters, roof flashing, hoods etc.

A] Galvanised iron

B] Stainless steel

C] Copper sheet

D] Metal sheets

2-142] in dairies. food processing, kitchen ware etc.

A] Galvanised iron

B] Stainless steel

C] Copper sheet

D] Metal sheets

3-143] for making buckets, heating ducts, cabinets etc.

A] Galvanised iron

B] Stainless steel

C] Copper sheet

D] Metal sheets

4-144] in canneries and chemical plants Metal sheets

A] Galvanised iron

B] Stainless steel

C] Copper sheet

D] Metal sheets

5-145] Ammonium chloride is used as a flux for soldering...

A] steel
B] aluminium
C] galvanized iron
D] stainless steel

6-146] Soldering of M.S sheets takes place at a temperature of...
A] 150?C
B] 250?C
C] 400?C
D] 850?C

7-147.] In soldering operation the base metal is...
A.] not heated
B.] heated to 200?C
C.] heated to 650?C
D.] heated to red hot condition

8-148] Rivets for Joining sheets to thick plates.
A] Countersunk head
B] Flat head
C] Pan head
D] Mushroom

9-149] Rivets for Joining sheet metal.
A] Countersunk head
B] Flat head
C] Pan head
D] Mushroom

10-150] Rivets for Heavy fabrication work.
A] Countersunk head
B] Flat head
C] Pan head
D] Mushroom

INDUSTRIAL TRAINING INSTITUTE

Monthly Test-11, Marks- 20, Date:- ______________

(Every Question Carry Two Marks)

1-156] The peak-to-peak voltage is 99V. how big is the effective value of the sine wave?
A] 70 V
B] 44.5V
C] 49.5 V
D] 35 V

2-157] A moving coil voltmeter reads 10 V AC. How big is the effective voltage?

A] higher

B] lower

C] the same

D] 10% higher

3-158] A moving iron ammeter reads 10 A. how big is the peak current of the oscillation?

A] 7.07 A

B] 1.1414A

C] 70.7 A

D] 14.1 A

4-159] A current of 2 amps flows through a resistance of 10 ohms. The power dissipated in the resistance is equal to...

A. 20 watts

B. 200 watts

C. 40 watts

D. 5 watts

5-160] Power companies are interested in improving the power factor to

A] reduce line current

B] increase motor efficiency

C] increase volt-amperes

D] decrease power

6-161.] Moving coil instrument works on the effect of...

A] chemical effect

B] heating effect

C] electrostatic effect

D] electromagnetic effect

7-162] The angle of below pipe to the line of weld in leftward welding technique is...

A] 40 to 50?

B] 50 to 60?

C] 60 to 70?

D. 70 to 80?

8-163] The angle of filler rod in case of rightward welding technique is...

A] 10 to 20?

B] 20 to 30?

C] 30 to 40?

D] 40 to 50?

9-164] Forge welding is classified as...

A] Fusion welding without pressure

B] Fusion welding with pressure

C] Non-fusion welding without pressure

D] no-fusion welding with pressure

10-165] One of the functions of flux in gas welding is...

A] Dissolve the metal oxides

B] Reduce the melting point of mental

C] Increase the flame temperature

D] Increase the root penetration

INDUSTRIAL TRAINING INSTITUTE

Monthly Test-12, Marks- 20, Date:- ______________

(Every Question Carry Two Marks)

1-171] Acetylene gas contains

A] Calcium, carbon and hydrogen

B] Calcium and hydrogen

C] Calcium, carbon, hydrogen and oxygen

D] Carbon and hydrogen

2-172] In an acetylene purifier the sulphureted and phosphorated hydrogen are removed by...

A] Pumice

B] Water

C] Filter wool

D] Purifying chemicals

3-173] Maximum temperature for forging H. S. S. is ------------degree.

A] 1200

B] 100

C] 1100

D] 1500

4-174] Main purpose Of annealing is -----------.

A] To improve machinability

B] To improve magnetism

C] To increase hardness

D] To increase toughness

5-175] The carbon percentage in H.S.S. tool is -------

A] 0.75 to 1.00 %

B] 1.00 to 2.00 00

C] 0.60 to 0.75 %

D] 0.02 to 0.03 %.

6-176] Which one of the following is the resistance of a metal to elastic deformation?

A] Ductility.

B] Strength

C] Stiffness

D] Toughness

7-177] The process of heating and cooling to change the structure of steel for obtaining the required properties is called

A] Hardening

B] Normalizing

C] Heat treatment

D] Tempering

8-178] The main purpose of annealing is to

A] Increase the hardness

B] Increase the toughness

C] Improve machinability

D] Improve distortion

9-179] The purpose of normalizing steel is to -----------

A] Remove the induced Stress

B] Improve genes and reduce brittleness

C] Soften the metal

D] Increase the surface?

10-180] Which one of the following process is used for hardenmg the outer 5" Annealing

A] Hardening

B] Tempering

C] Case Hardening

D] Tear surface

www.ingramcontent.com/pod-product-compliance
Ingram Content Group UK Ltd.
Pitfield, Milton Keynes, MK11 3LW, UK
UKHW021919190726
13853UKWH00002B/744

9 798888 696569